Visions of Hope

.

Visions of Hope

Reflections for Chronic Patients
Based on the Stations of the Cross

EVA DÉLI
with MARK O'MALLEY

Illustrations by Eva Déli

Foreword by Glenn L. Monson

RESOURCE *Publications* • Eugene, Oregon

Resource Publications
An Imprint of Wipf and Stock Publishers
199 W. 8th Ave., Suite 3
Eugene, OR 97401

www.wipfandstock.com

PAPERBACK ISBN: 978-1-7252-7003-9
HARDCOVER ISBN: 978-1-7252-7004-6
EBOOK ISBN: 978-1-7252-6995-8

Manufactured in the U.S.A. 05/21/20

To my Parents, József Déli and Etelka Hudák

Contents

List of Poetry

Foreword

It is rare that one reads a book where religion and science are not at odds, if not warring altogether. Religious folks call into question the assumptions and assertions of scientists. Similarly, scientists call into question the assumptions and assertions of religionists. What a delight it is to read an author who has the insight and wisdom to appreciate the gifts of both. Indeed Eva Deli has not only the rare ability to appreciate both, but the ability to understand in some depth how each discipline can coexist with the other and provide a healing balm to all who are on the journey of life-threatening illness. She is clearly both a fine scientist and a person of faith, who seeks to bring a word of healing, understanding, and compassion to a suffering world.

Eva Deli is also an artist, and perhaps this is where her gifts are most evident. I first encountered Eva's artistry when she exhibited the Stations at my parish in Austin, Minnesota during a Holy Week observance. People came and viewed the stations, reflected on their meaning for them, said prayers, and departed, I believe, with a stronger sense of what the Suffering Christ experienced.

The connection Eva makes between the Stations and the progression of a terminal illness is remarkable and shows her artistic insight. From Station 1, where Jesus is condemned though innocent, through Station XIV, where Jesus is laid in the tomb, we see a remarkably accurate parallel to what the "stations" of a terminal illness are. There is no manipulation of the Stations to see how the "stations" of a terminal illness fit precisely with the experience of Jesus' journey to Golgotha.

When Jesus is condemned, though innocent, is that not the experience of one who receives a terminal diagnosis? We ask, "But what have I done to deserve this?" The assumed answer is, "Nothing. You are innocent." The thrice falling of Jesus also is uncannily like the setbacks which are so common in a patient's journey. One day we feel stronger, the disease seems to be in remission, and the next, another tumor appears and we "fall" again. The persons who assist Jesus, from his mother to Simon, to Veronica, also seem very familiar. Family and friends, physicians and nurses, and yes, strangers too, provide the care and encouragement that are so important at each "station" of the journey. Even the experience of death, which begins with being parted from our earthly possessions, pictured as Jesus being stripped of his garments, and ends with our death, pictured in Jesus' death on the Cross, fits our experience so well.

This book is a gift to anyone looking for meaning and peace during the journey of terminal illness. The religious quotes are abundant, as is counsel in how to manage one's thoughts and emotions during this torturous yet holy time. The insights of Eva Deli the artist, the scientist, the philosopher, and the religionist are all present here and offered with humility, generosity and grace.

Glenn Monson PhD, Senior Pastor at Mount Olive Lutheran Church, author of "Afflicting the Comfortable, Comforting the Afflicted: A Guide to Law and Gospel Preaching"

Preface

> "When you come to the end of all the light you
> know, and it's time to step into the darkness of the
> unknown, faith is knowing that one of two things shall
> happen: Either you will be given something solid to
> stand on, or you will be taught to fly."
>
> —EDWARD TELLER

Throughout human history, the perception of a disease often reflected superstition and a lack of awareness. In the Middle Ages, epidemics were viewed as a punishment of sins. This notion is echoed in the gospel of John 9:2–3 (NIV) "Who sinned, this man or his parents, that he was born blind?" In his response, Jesus dispels prejudices and fear. "Neither this man nor his parents sinned, but this happened so that the works of God might be displayed in him." Patients with AIDS, diabetes, cancer, and other chronic diseases are still in need of His wisdom. This is especially true for the highly emotional period following the diagnosis, which tests the relationship dynamics with family and friends.

Following the Second World War, a better understanding of human physiology, the discovery of DNA, vaccinations, and other breakthrough research led to optimism and belief in the power of modern medicine. The appearance of novel diseases, such as AIDS, SARS, ebola, and others, has poured cold water on that optimism. Although chemotherapy, radiation, immunotherapy, and surgery substantially extended the survival of cancer patients, the complexity of the underlying mechanisms has made progress in treatment more challenging than initially thought. The increasing life expectancy and the unintended consequences of our modern technologies have also increased the prevalence of certain cancers. Western-style medicine has also been confounded by the psychological side effects of chronic conditions. Everyone has lost uncles, aunts, other family members, and friends to cancer, AIDS, or other chronic diseases. These losses are always painful.

Cancer was brought home to me while attending a benefit concert for a friend diagnosed with brain cancer. It inspired me to view the illness through the lens of Stations of the Cross. The Stations of the Cross are a Christian tradition about Jesus' last hours of humiliation and horrendous suffering before his execution on Golgotha. This was in 2005; I had just completed a paper collage series on the Stations. In light of my friend's declining health, the haunting images of the Stations acquired a new meaning of the tortuous trajectory of chronic diseases. My motivation to present the Stations in a book form was solidified ten years later, after watching my mother's health slowly decline and succumb to multiple myeloma, a type of cancer.

How could the events that happened two thousand years ago carry a special meaning for chronic patients today? In Jesus' time, death was a regular part and parcel of the brutal struggle for survival. There was no opportunity for the patients or their families to contemplate the emotional and psychological consequences of their conditions. For patients, recognizing the parallels in the disease process with Jesus' trials in the Stations can be highly rewarding and comforting.

The Stations of the Cross starts out with Pilate condemning Jesus to death and ends with his burial in a tomb. The tradition is based on Jesus' original path on the Via Dolorosa in Jerusalem to Mount Calvary. Beginning in the 15th and 16th centuries, the reenactment of the Stations allowed believers to meditate over Jesus' profoundly human experience of suffering. This meaningful practice is still alive within the Catholic community. The reenactment in the Colosseum of Rome became a worldwide television event; the Pope himself used to carry the cross.

Jesus suffers three increasingly difficult falls on his route to crucifixion. Each fall symbolizes his increasing weariness, pain, and dependence on others. The first fall represents the confused, disoriented state following diagnosis and its initial setbacks. The second fall is the depression and discouragement brought about by the side effects of chemotherapy, surgery, etc. and their toll on the human body. This includes the sequelae of the disease, such as secondary tumors, infections, and the associated stress, depression, and other problems. The third fall symbolizes the physical and mental exhaustion that precedes the acceptance of death.

Yet, during the months and years of the disease progression, the patient attempts to live a "normal" existence. Simon, who only has an accidental connection to Jesus, represents the medical community and relationships with the broader society. Veronika symbolizes the support of friends and strangers during the loneliness of the disease. Jesus' meeting with his mother is a metaphor for family connections. Jesus comforts his female followers with compassion and dignity. Likewise, sometimes the patient's courage and fortitude console his desperate friends and family.

The final stations provide mental and emotional transformations in the face of death. Accepting our mortality enhances the appreciation for the meaning of life. The empowering state of surrender eliminates fear, which can positively influence the course of the disease. Being placed in the tomb is a metaphor for our limitations, our mortality, and the questions of an afterlife. The last station, not part of the original series, is hope. Hope is inherent in every human being and even in every living creature. Life, especially for those with chronic disease, withers without sustaining inspiration.

The following pages acknowledge the crucial importance of the three overarching human disciplines to aid in healing. Religion, the arts, and sciences can work together to serve the body and the soul. Their complementarity is the best assurance to manage the physical, spiritual, and emotional components of healing. The images and the poetry that accompany the thought-provoking message of the text encourage contemplation and meditation. As one progresses through the disease, each station can take on new meaning. Therefore it might be rewarding to revisit the artwork, the text, and the poetry. I hope you find this multifaceted work an inspiring journey toward self-discovery and healing.

Acknowledgments

Working on a book without financial security can be a daunting challenge. What I found is that immersing myself with trust in my family, friends, and social circle miraculously brought me the help I needed.

One of my closest friends, Susan M. Radloff, invited me to live in a spare bedroom of her stately home.

I am thankful for Glenn Monson for consultations on theology and other matters.

Terrance Norman Dilley searched for appropriate poetry for the chapters.

Dr. Mark O'Malley corrected my imprecise phrases and expertly wove the medical information into the text without overwhelming the reader with medical jargon.

Gregory A. Kiss went through the text with a fine comb to find my grammar mistakes.

The Institute of Noetic Sciences gave kind permission for the use of the exhaustive list on spontaneous remissions of cancer, authored by O'Regan & Hirshberg.

The encouragement by Virginia Larson, Susan M. Radloff, Linda Machka, and many others was instrumental in bringing this book to completion.

Abbreviations

New International Version (NIV)
New King James Version (NKJV)
English Standard Version (ESV)
New Living Translation (NLT)
Good News Translation (GNT)

STATION I

Jesus Is Condemned

"Preserve me, o God: for in thee do I put my trust."
—Psalm 16:1 (KJV)

1, JUDGEMENT: DIAGNOSIS OF THE DISEASE

"People about to embark on an illness journey have
not been prepared for even the most basic pragmatic
or emotional adaptations they will have to make."

—ANGELA ARMSTRONG-COSTNER[1]

"We want the facts to fit the preconceptions. When
they don't it is easier to ignore the facts than to change
the preconceptions."

—JESSAMYN WEST

"I have come to believe that caring for myself is not
self-indulgent. Caring for myself is an act of survival."

—AUDRE LORDE

Pilate, the governor of Judea, condemns Jesus to death. Over and
over, Pilate declares to the mob that Jesus is innocent: "'What shall
I do, then, with Jesus who is called the Messiah?' Pilate asked.
They all answered, 'Crucify him!' 'Why? What crime has he com-
mitted?' asked Pilate. But they shouted all the louder, 'Crucify
him!'" Matt. 27:22–23 (NIV).

The Gospels make it very clear that Jesus actively chose to accept his fate. This unyielding commitment is not requested from
us. Modern medicine often spares us from a torturous and quick
passing. Recovery and longer-term survival are possible in an increasing number of diseases that used to be death sentences, even
less than a decade ago. Thanks to a series of treatment options
administered over many months or years, people with a terminal
illness can survive and enjoy many years of active life.

The diagnosis of a terminal disease is a severe and disorient-
ing blow that can trigger endless self-examination. The cold and
often foreign words of the diagnosis prompt the question, "What

1. Armstrong-Costner, *Living and Dying with Cancer*, 33.

have I done to deserve this?" The trauma is overwhelming. The loss of invincibility parallels the betrayal and condemnation of Jesus. Genetics, environmental exposure, and the biological lottery fail to give us an emotionally satisfying answer. It is more meaningful to blame the disease on a preordained destiny or some past traumatic event. Such contemplations reflect the intuitive belief in karma, which implies that our life represents the visible surface of some deeper forces. In Eastern philosophy, karma, the idea that the intent and actions of an individual (cause) influence the future of that individual (effect), is a crucial concept.

In the Gospels, several examples refer to karma, such as Galatians 6:7 (NIV). Luke 8:17 writes, "For there is nothing hidden that will not be disclosed; nothing concealed that will not be known or brought out into the open." While many illnesses can be blamed on heredity or environmental factors, most often, these investigations remain futile. Getting through the first painful shock of being face-to-face with death triggers a change of habits and beliefs; it forces a reevaluation of relationships and a way of life.

The recognition of our mortality triggers grief, anguish that can be debilitating but also can lead to catharsis. The latter is a transformative process that incorporates the ability to accept irreversible changes into our mental fabric. A spontaneous self-cross-examination actively and meaningfully weaves the changed reality into our present. This slow emotional process formulates a positive vision about the future.

The grieving process was studied by Elisabeth Kübler-Ross[2] in her 1969 book, *On Death and Dying*. She found that there are five stages of grief, varying in duration and sequence.

1. Denial and isolation; blocking out the meaning of the diagnosis can numb emotional reactions and hide the painful facts from awareness.
2. Anger, confusion, and overwhelming pain can culminate in resentment: "why me, why did I get this?"
3. Bargaining and self-blame: "If only I sought medical attention sooner . . . if only I had done things differently."

2. Kubler-Ross, *On Death and Dying*.

4. Depression, chaos, and self-deprecation seem to crash down on the patient.

5. Acceptance; acceptance and submission are calm, retrospective, and emotionally stable conditions. They are necessary for the peaceful and dignified transition to death. They are also conducive to making peace with the treatments, social, and family dynamics. Acceptance also provides a path for better disease management and healing.

As our physical body depends on stability, our wellbeing craves mental balance. The unsettling emotional and physical facets of the disease unbalance the mind. Our innate drive to restore psychological balance is an emergency mechanism, called stress. Stress can have both positive and negative impacts. Its positive effect is that it makes you aware and careful in dangerous situations. Chronic stress inhibits healing because it blocks the brain's automatic ability to orient with changing circumstances. In chronic illness, the emotional rollercoaster of stressful states can trigger fear.

Fear is an organic part of the disease process. Like a flashlight that exposes only a small slice of the environment, anxiety is a focus on a small, highly detailed section of reality, such as symptoms of the illness. Trust, like a chandelier that illuminates the whole room, provides a coherent picture. When you trust, you can remain objectively detached from your disease. Objectivity permits a mental order about your treatment options, which highly increases your confidence and emotional stability. Active participation can motivate a more disciplined treatment regimen and the efficiency of the protocol.

Emotions reflect our complex relationships within the physical and social world. Because we continuously identify with our emotions, they form the basis of our intellect and an inherent part of our psyche. Bodily changes accompany emotions. For example, the tightening of the throat correlates with the feeling of pressure and suffocation, whereas relaxing of the body gives rise to a sense of expansion. We feel heavy during remorse, arguments are exhausting, and have almost limitless energy during awe and happiness.

Observing bodily reactions during emotional moments replace their self-centered aspect with a profoundly empowering
outside view. Such a comprehensive insight into the subjective and
highly partial perspective of our soul endows the bodily experience with understanding and meaning. Perceiving the location and
physiological manifestation of physical or emotional pain lessens
its subjective bite. It is temporary, but empowering relief. Taking
your illness with all its ramifications liberates your mind's natural
resilience for healing. Understanding our emotions is the first deci-
sive step to gaining control over the disease process.

GIVE ME STRENGTH

This is my prayer to thee, my lord—strike,
strike at the root of penury in my heart.

Give me the strength lightly to bear my joys and sorrows.

Give me the strength to make my love fruitful in service.

Give me the strength never to disown the poor or bend my knees before insolent might.

Give me the strength to raise my mind high above daily trifles.

And give me the strength to surrender my strength to thy will with love.

By Rabindranath Tagore

"WHEN I AM AFRAID, I PUT MY TRUST IN YOU." PSALM 56:3 | NIV

When you pass through the waters,
I will be with you;
and when you pass through the rivers,
they will not sweep over you.
When you walk through the fire,
you will not be burned;
the flames will not set you ablaze.

    Isaiah 43:2 | NIV

STATION II

Jesus Takes up His Cross

"Then he called the crowd to him along with his
disciples and said: 'Whoever wants to be my disciple
must deny themselves and take up their cross
and follow me.'"

—MARK 8:34 (NIV)

2, BECOMING FAMILIAR WITH THE DISEASE

"Truly I tell you, if you have faith and do not doubt
. . . you can say to this mountain, 'Go, throw yourself
into the sea,' and it will be done. If you believe, you will
receive whatever you ask for in prayer."

—MATTHEW: 21:21–22 (NIV)

"It is during our darkest moments that we must focus
to see the light."

—ARISTOTLE

"I have learned to live each day as it comes, and not to
borrow trouble by dreading tomorrow. It is the dark
menace of the future that makes cowards of us."

—DOROTHY DIX

Jesus takes up his cross. The condemned man must carry his torture and death penalty device to Golgotha (the Place of a Skull). Jesus has already endured scourging at the hands of the soldiers, which must have weakened him. Although we don't know much about his state of mind, he must have been under considerable mental and emotional strain. His painful and demeaning death on the cross makes his innocence all the more apparent. He had to cross the bowels of hell to provide a way for us to heaven.

The seemingly endless labyrinth of the disease parallels with Jesus' torturous walk to Golgotha. Philippians 2:5–8 reflects this well: "Let the same mind be in you that was in Christ Jesus, who, though he was in the form of God, did not regard equality with God as something to be exploited, but emptied himself, taking the form of a slave, being born in human likeness. And being found in human form, he humbled himself and became obedient to the point of death—even death on a cross." Witnessing Jesus' victimhood makes the cross a timeless symbol. Believers often honor his sacrifice by wearing the cross as jewelry. Meditating and praying over the special meaning of the Stations can help to redefine your disease situation as well.

Educating yourself about the illness is essential. A thorough understanding of the disease and treatment options, as well as their side effects, can strengthen the will to live. Familiarity with the treatment options and their possible outcomes encourages a partnership with the medical team. The collaboration reinforces your confidence and increases your trust in the process. Just as physical laws govern a rock's flight to its impact on the windowpane, your disease path will be determined by genetics, the current state of medicine, and even the air you breathe. There is one factor that you are absolutely in control of: your state of mind. Positive reframing of your disease situation reduces distress. The emotions you form today will modulate your stress level and healing tomorrow. The plan developed by you, your family, and the medical team will have a set of goals that need to be met and from time-to-time need to be modified. Making a conscious choice about treatment options such as surgery, chemo, and immunotherapy, we actively "take up the cross."

Formulating goals is a powerful motivation and a crucial step in triggering your body's will to manage the disease. The loss of security and safety due to disease serves as an opportunity to reflect on your life and set uplifting goals. Patients who set goals tend to live past significant milestones in their lives, such as the birth of a grandchild or their spouse's birthday. The mind will focus the body's energies toward such comprehensible personal and therapeutic goals; it is a victory of the human will, spirit, and social connectedness.

Choosing meaningful goals at the time of diagnosis will inspire your energies and carry you forward. Goals and social networks (even our pets!) can provide emotional sustenance, inspiration, and interest in life. Science has yet to find an explanation for the personal ability to concentrate life's energies that way.

Biological, physiological needs, circadian rhythms, and even environmental circumstances influence performance toward your objectives (goals). The mind projects expectations for the future and constructs action steps. Mental fluidity depends on the brain's energy distribution and turnover. When we are tired and hungry, we become superficial, impatient, and sloppy. Confusion is an antagonistic, angry, and desperate state. Stress degrades trust, and determination. It can cause disturbances on the molecular level, leading to immune problems. Keeping the past free of disappointments, emotional pains, and mental chaos crystalizes your purpose.

Writing down your goals, plans, and your observations can minimize your stress. Jotting down even little tidbits of insight and information will chart your progress, and it will sharpen your focus. Keeping a journal is also helpful to the medical team. Compiling thoughts this way can weave even tiny slivers of insight into a complex idea and wisdom. Keep evaluating your emotional progress in the weeks, months, and years to come. Regularly correcting your course will steady your commitment without falling into complacency. You must have the willingness to make changes if new circumstances require.

When my mother was diagnosed with cancer, I moved in with her to work on my first book. Her crowded house needed substantial cleaning. Progressing with the chore came at the price of neglecting my writing. The disease environment, the housework, and taking care of my mother had planted doubts in my mind about my abilities to finish my book. My misgivings led to excuses to postpone and question my commitment. Everybody has a mental limit, a subconscious set point, based on our experience and expectations. To renew my focus required a conscious decision to rededicate myself to my work.

People who fail in life often place blame on insurmountable challenges, their past, or even their childhood. To be successful requires us to overcome the difficulties we are handed. To make steel, you have to challenge the iron. "As iron sharpens iron, so one person sharpens another," we read in Proverbs 27:17 (NIV). Acceptance of your disease and your conscious choices increase your sense of power and belief in a positive outcome.

The Power of Acceptance

"Clothe yourselves with compassion,
kindness, humility, gentleness and patience."

—COLOSSIANS 3:12 (NIV)

"Be completely humble and gentle;
be patient, bearing with one another in love."

—EPHESIANS 4:2 (NIV)

"Humble yourselves before the Lord,
and he will lift you up."

—JAMES 4:10 (NIV)

Our opinions are rooted in our morals, values, and principles. Our internal model represents our expectations of how the world should work. Setbacks serve as robust criticism that invalidates our closely held ideas; even compliments can trigger our insecurities. Partiality shuts down the mind for acceptance. Such bias necessitates the need to protect the self, to be defensive against every fleeting negative experience. A closed, narrow viewpoint is a mental prison, which steals our ability for healing.

The brain's limited energy supply influences its ability to relate to the environment. Clinging to obsolete information robs precious time and energy, and wreaks havoc on the hormonal and immune system. Feedback and suggestions from others are the best opportunities to change and grow. Listening attentively is a sign of respect that serves a much-needed second perspective. Considering advice allows us to see ourselves through the eyes of others. Meditating on suggestions in our own time is most beneficial. "Never react emotionally to criticism. Analyze yourself to determine whether it is justified. If it is, correct yourself. Otherwise, go on about your business," writes Norman Vincent Peale.

Just as Jesus accepted his fate, we must accept ours. When we are occupied by worry and regret, we fail to take care of the present, which forwards the problems into the future. Although it takes focused and persistent work, we can change our beliefs and eliminate negative attitudes. Some useful strategies are listed in Station VI. Acceptance of your disease can give way to an inherently positive journey. Although it requires effort, it liberates immense mental power. "One's suffering disappears when one lets oneself go when one yields—even to sadness," says Antoine de Saint-Exeupéry. Like switching a car into gear, acceptance suddenly changes your attitude and corrects your mental course. The resulting mental flexibility is conducive to healing.

Humbleness is not a weakness but a form of an embrace, which allows you to view a problem with positive mental energy. Because our future is the continuation of our past, a negative focus curtails our options via rigidity. Negative emotions manifest as distrust and excuses, which triggers the flight or fight reaction. Either fight or flight reflects the inability to accept what cannot be changed and weakens confidence and determination. Reevaluating your situation permits you to find the hopeful aspects that allow progress. Acceptance allows you to step out of the confinement and the tight grip of stress. Your natural buoyancy will be liberated. The more difficult issues you are fighting, the more significant uplift the process produces.

Acceptance lacks pride, it is modest and humble. It is generous and congruent with the essence of things. It is an energetic state, which enables understanding and permits natural solutions; it is the beauty of clarity, which leads to coherence and transparency. It negates the need to be defensive, and even works retrospectively. Giving up your hold on the past increases mental freedom, and points you toward the future. Spiritual cleansing reappraises the problem, which eliminates self-serving bias, envy, resentment, and self-pity. It introduces a broader, relaxed perspective, allowing a powerful path toward progress.

The environment, the universe, and the wisdom of God shape the mind. The more you mirror your God with honesty and genuineness, the more care and sustenance the universe will provide to you. Your only duty is to express and manifest your Self, your unique role, and purpose in life. This gift and opportunity come with a responsibility to live out your full potential. Jesus also emphasized the power of contentment in the connectedness with God.

Sacrifice empowers you. When giving selflessly, then your emotional state does not depend on the outcome. Having no regrets liberates from negativity. The open mind gives one the courage to ask, and the humbleness to accept help. Doing everything with a full heart and without expectation eliminates regret, and it helps to achieve peace and clarity. People who work toward the betterment of others and themselves are more confident and have better disease outcomes. Working against your internal resistance and putting others ahead of your own needs will lead to resentment and regret. These reactive emotions destroy the ability to engage, relate to others and situations via trust, and find natural solutions.

As energy flows from warmer to colder matter, emotionally stable people tend to gather wisdom and meaning from every experience. Thus, emotional stability—the ability to hold back impulsivity—goes a long way toward individual wellbeing and social cooperation. A positive outlook turns negative experiences into wisdom because the light of understanding reveals the good that is in the shadow. When we trust our soul, we open up toward the possibilities of the future, the wisdom of existence.

The most significant promise for yourself is to feel the joy of existence every single day. When you have unbridled happiness, then you find the world beautiful, open, and accepting. That is an innocent, childlike state of wonder.

ALL THINGS

are too small to hold me, I am SO vast
In the Infinite I reach for the Uncreated
I have touched it, it undoes me wider than wide
Everything else
is too narrow
You know this well, you who are also there

By Hadewijck II 13th century

THREE FRIENDS

OF all the blessings which my life has known,
I value most, and most praise God for three:
Want, Loneliness and Pain, those comrades true,
Who, masqueraded in the garb of foes
For many a year, and filled my heart with dread.
Yet fickle joys, like false, pretentious friends,
Have proved less worthy than this trio. First,
Want taught me labor, led me up the steep
And toilsome paths to hills of pure delight,
Trod only by the feet that know fatigue,
And yet press on until the heights appear.
Then loneliness and hunger of the heart
Sent me upreaching to the realms of space,
Till all the silences grew eloquent,
And all their loving forces hailed me friend.
Last, pain taught prayer! placed in my hand the staff
Of close communion with the over-soul,
That I might lean upon it to the end,
And find myself made strong for any strife.
And then these three who had pursued my steps
Like stern, relentless foes, year after year,
Unmasked, and turned their faces full on me,
And lo! they were divinely beautiful,
For through them shone the lustrous eyes of Love.
    By Ella Wheeler Wilcox

STATION III

Jesus Falls for the First Time

"Be not far from me; for trouble is near;
For there is none to help."

—Psalm 22:11 (NIV)

3, INITIAL SETBACKS, THE FEELING OF LOSS

"Be careful what you think,
because your thoughts run your life."

—PROVERBS 4:23 (NCV)

"Fix your thoughts on what is true, and honorable, and
right, and pure, and lovely, and admirable. Think about
things that are excellent and worthy of praise."

—PHILIPPIANS 4:8 (NLT)

"Disbelief may act as a barrier . . . to healing.
[In other words], disbelief and healing
cannot exist in the same plane."

—CAITLIN MATTHEWS

Under the Roman system, the condemned were often required to carry the cross piece on which they would be crucified. Jesus' falling under the weight of his cross underscores his solidarity with all those who suffer. By sharing in our suffering, he gave us a hope to share in his grace as well. "We have [Jesus] who in every respect has been tested as we are, yet without sin. Let us, therefore, approach the throne of grace with boldness, so that we may receive mercy and find grace to help in time of need," writes Hebrews 4:15–16 (NIV).

Regular checkups often become part of life for cancer, heart disease, AIDS, or diabetes patients. During these checkups, we may receive bad news: the tumor is not shrinking, the labs are not normalizing. The chemotherapy, radiation, and surgical aftereffects can lead to a sense of altered body image. Because our sense of self is tightly interwoven with our body image, the physical changes can cause insecurity and psychological problems. Loss of a limb, hair loss, skin changes, weight loss or gain, anxiety, depression—these are just a few of the transformations experienced by the patient.

Friends, family, or colleagues can have a hard time understanding the inner turmoil.

The above examples are just some of the initial setbacks seen in chronic diseases. The difficulties trigger deep-seated emotions: the fear of the outcome, the physical and emotional pain, and the unknowable loneliness of the condition. Patients of chronic diseases often cannot participate in social life and often feel excluded from it. The emotional scars of invasive treatments also enhance the pain of this separation. According to Albert Schweitzer, the shared outcast status is "the mark of the brotherhood of pain." Buddha cuts to the core of anxiety: "If the problem can be solved why worry? If the problem cannot be solved, worrying will do you no good." A similar sentiment is expressed by Apostle Paul in Philippians 4:11 (NLT): "I have learned to be content with whatever I have."

The disease can degrade the will, but it can also lead to growth and insights in perseverance. It can serve as an opportunity to find blessings and new meaning in life. Norman Cousins, an author and professor, was diagnosed with a rare degenerative illness at the age of fifty. He was given only a few months to live by his doctors, but he refused to accept his fate. His book, *Anatomy of an Illness*, is a testimony of the health benefits of positive emotions and laughter, which probably cured him. The art of comedy can dissolve stress. Positive emotions boost immune function, blood flow, and resilience by improving connective complexity in the brain.

Our capacity for happiness depends on the ability to bounce back from stressful situations. Accompanying the therapeutic options with mind-body and spirit enhancing practices boosts their healing power. Emotionally secure people are more likely to respond positively to crises in their lives. There is a well-founded positive relationship between spirituality and well-being. Such appreciation lends a vision about the interdependence and interconnectedness of life. The uplifting emotional outlet of interactions with God through prayer is particularly pronounced in chronic conditions, such as cancer.

Positive appraisals soften the negative inducing nature of stress. Strive for a positive reframing of your situation. Gratitude is a positive mindset, which improves the ability to cope with setbacks and reduces the chances of side effects. It decreases depression symptoms over the long-term. It protects us from the destructive impulses of envy, resentment, greed, and bitterness and it helps us to effectively cope with everyday stress. Gratitude improves life satisfaction and physical and mental health. It boosts positive emotions, such as joy, enthusiasm, love, happiness, and optimism. Writing a gratitude journal can improve sleep quality, which is particularly important in the later stages of the disease. Grateful people are rated by others as more helpful, outgoing, optimistic, and trustworthy. This takes us to the section on placebos.

The Power of the Placebo

"I would rather know the person who has the disease than the disease the person has."

—HIPPOCRATES

"Do something today that your future self will thank you for."

—SEAN PATRICK FLANERY

Two thousand five hundred years ago, in the battle of Marathon, the massively outnumbered Greek soldiers took a stand against the invading Persian army. One of the defenders ran on foot to Athens, 42 km away, to notify the city-state about the defeat of the Persians. After he delivered his message of victory, he collapsed and died. His heroism inspired the Marathon race. More importantly, the story is perhaps the most eloquent illustration of the power of the mind. There are many documented cases of superhuman feats, such as when people momentarily can lift immense weight to save someone's life, win a battle against powerful foes or spontaneous remissions of tumors. These notable achievements and healings cannot be easily explained by science. The above examples show the intertwined relationship between our faculties, health, medical condition, and the mind. Motivation can overcome the physical limitations of the body. If we crystallize our courage, our bodies will follow along to bring forth satisfaction and healing.

Significant advancements in surgical techniques, medications, and other regimens have transformed modern medicine. Nevertheless, the accompanying side effects of illnesses such as depression, chronic pain, anxiety, and fatigue, have been challenging for traditional medicine to address. The psychological conditions, such as chronic pain, and fatigue, can determine the disease prognosis. For example, doctors and nurses can often tell at the first meeting whether the patient will get better or succumb to the disease. Subjective variation in responses to the same treatment regimen led researchers to consider the power of the mind in healing.

Placebo is Latin for "I will please." It is considered as a sham medication or procedure designed to be void of any known therapeutic value. The placebo effect can have both objective and subjective properties. Although it appears to have a substantial genetic component (objective), its overall therapeutic value is due to the patient's views about the treatments rather than the treatment itself (subjective side). Placebos positively influence effectiveness, whereas nocebo is a harmful outcome.

How can we harness the power of the placebo? Our life pulses to the rhythm of our securities. When we feel confident, we make wise decisions, but anxiety brings forth mistakes and accidents. Creating the best possible environment for healing signals your commitment to recovery. An openness toward the present experiences, separate from pain and discomfort, might allow smaller doses of the drug to be effective. A can-do attitude indicates to society that you are taking charge of your disease. It boosts the morale of your medical team, friends, and relatives and encourages them to become active participants in your recovery with help, advice, and encouragement. Emotional stability, which permits confidence, is not the lack of negative emotions in the present but reducing or eliminating their long-term consequences.

Diet, Exercise and the Mind-body Connection

Positive changes in diet and exercise habits boost the body's innate resilience. Healthy eating habits serve the spirit as well. The recent discovery that the gut microbiome can modulate brain function and behaviors relevant to anxiety and depression gives new meaning to the adage "you are what you eat." Adopt a diet that serves your needs and aligns with healing. The discipline to submit to a particular regimen creates regular order, which increases your confidence and self-respect. A healthy regime creates a stable framework for strong motivation. After all, your disease path is formed by the way you live every day. Real and systematic life-changes can rejuvenate the mental world. Even small positive steps can have a profound influence on how you feel.

Without weight-bearing movement, we lose muscle mass. Chronic diseases can cause a similar weakening of the muscle system. Recent research shows that these changes not only weaken the body but also disrupt the biochemistry of the nervous system. One of the most powerful, clinically supported positive impacts on recovery is exercise. Exercise improves immune function and strengthens the body. It can trigger the creation of new neurons and form a positive influence on memory and executive function. Because the signals sent by the muscles to the brain influence mental health, it releases feel-good hormones. By improving mental and physical performance, it can stop and even reverse the physical decline of the disease. It is a gift of life functionality and mental agility.

In your mind, you carry the reflection of God, the whole universe. Considering your soul as a unique, essential part of the cosmic reality will permit you to view your body as a sacred creation. You are a beautiful, wholesome human being who deserves to be cherished, respected, and loved. It is your first job to live according to that truth by serving your mental and bodily health. When you respect yourself, then your body can focus on health and recovery. *Just do it.*

IN THIS SHORT LIFE THAT ONLY LASTS AN HOUR (1292)

In this short Life that only lasts an hour
How much—how little—is within our power
By Emily Dickinson

ADVERSITY THEN STRENGTH

I did not understand at first touch
but it is that conflict in life
that has shaped me to who I am today
these strengths were once weaknesses
and this love was once hate
being a caged bird has revealed to me
the beauty of freedom
so if you wish to be successful
let yourself fail
if you wish to be loved
let yourself hurt

By Henry Wadsworth Longfellow

STATION IV

Jesus Meets His Mother

"Be pleased, O Lord, to deliver me:
O Lord, make haste to help me."

—Psalms 40:13 (NKJV)

4, APPROACHING FAMILY AND FRIENDS

"Therefore my heart is glad, and my glory rejoices:
my flesh also will rest in hope."

—PSALM 16; 9 (KJB)

"Anxiety weighs down the heart,
but a kind word cheers it up."

—PROVERBS 12:25 (NIV)

"If you hold to my teaching, you are truly
My disciples. Then you will know the truth,
and the truth will set you free."

—JOHN 8:31–32 (NIV)

The mother of Jesus is never far from the scene of the crucifixion. In this stage, we see her pour out her love onto her tortured, beaten son. A secure relationship with your creator permits healthy connections with romantic partners, family members, and close friends as well. Their healing presence fortifies your determination to actively improve your life circumstances. The spread of single households in the modern world often comes at the price of social connectedness. Persistent loneliness can cause cardiovascular, hormonal, and immune problems; it can be as threatening as cigarettes, excess alcohol, or obesity. The adverse health consequences are especially dangerous during this time when the family is the single most essential lifeline.

Twenty-five years ago, I was pregnant with my third child. I came down with an intestinal infection, which caused severe diarrhea. A potent antibiotic, which would have treated the problem was out of the question. Every day for eight months of pregnancy and ten months of nursing, I would invariably be miserable and exhausted by 10 a.m. Constant diarrhea and the resulting hemorrhoids depleted my physical and mental energies. I was depressed.

In my helplessness and isolation, I scarcely remembered my past and was not able to comprehend or even be interested in the future. Life became a blur of tentative actions to last until the next emergency that I came to expect.

When my son was ten months old, antibiotic treatment restored my health almost overnight. The difficulties of that year were manageable because of the closeness of my family. Intimate relationships are essential for life and become even more meaningful at the intersection of life and death. Our vulnerability nurtures our closeness with those dearest to us. Secure social connections with loved ones provide an emotional strength that ties the patient to the living.

Like threads in a fabric, the richness of existence depends on an essential interdependence of all the components. Missing threads weaken the textile and create a hole. Likewise, the disappearance of even the smallest element leaves an opening in society. In John Donne's words, "any man's death diminishes me, because I am involved in Mankind."

According to cancer physician David Smithers, the quality of the social milieu has a crucial role in healing. Your friends, family, and coworkers create a climate of moral support that can advocate on your behalf. In the Scriptures, the appeal to take care of one another is vivid in Romans 12:15 (ESV), "Rejoice with those who rejoice; weep with those who weep."

Since ancient times, people used the arts and religion to wash off the dust of every day and transcend onto a higher intellectual plane. Recognition of the regularity in the cycles of the natural environment formed our earliest belief systems and encouraged the beginning of worship. Religion and spirituality immerse the soul within the mysteries of the universe and society. Humanity has an innate hunger for meaning in every experience. Socrates reminds us that we must examine life to make it worth living. Sometimes a disease that brings death into a close-up view is the best inspiration to discover a more personal relationship to life.

STATION IV

IF ONLY WE UNDERSTOOD

Could we but draw back the curtains
That surround each other's lives,
See the naked heart and spirit,
Know what spur the action gives,
Often we should find it better
Purer than we judged we should,
We should love each other better,
If we only understood.
If we knew the cares and trials,
Knew the efforts all in vain,
And the bitter disappointment,
Understood the loss and gain—

Would the grim, eternal roughness
Seem—I wonder—just the same?
Should we help where now we hinder?
Should we pity where we blame?
Ah, we judge each other harshly,
Know not life's hidden force:
Knowing not the fount of action
Is less turbid at its source:
Seeing amid the evil
All the golden grain of good:
And we'd love each other better.
If we only understood.
	by Anonymous

STATION V

Simon the Cyrene Helps
Jesus Carry the Cross

"A joyful heart is good medicine,
but a crushed spirit dries up the bones."

—Proverbs 17:22 (ESV)

5, MEDICAL ENVIRONMENT

"Ask and it will be given to you; seek and you will find;
knock and the door will be opened to you."

—MATTHEW 7:7 (NIV)

"Carry each other's burdens, and in this way you will
fulfill the law of Christ."

—GALATIANS 6:2 (NIV)

Simon of Cyrene is a stranger and a passerby. On the orders of the soldiers, he helps Jesus to carry his cross to Golgotha. His involuntary involvement lightens Jesus' burden. We do not know if Simon had compassion for Jesus, or was simply afraid to disobey the soldiers. Nevertheless, he eased Jesus' sense of isolation. The taunting, weeping crowds, and the soldiers' merciless orders that drove the procession must have deeply affected him. How much did he understand about Jesus' ministry?

The effectiveness of the treatment highly depends on the patient's subjective sense of safety and security. Modern care is increasingly centered on these. Compassionate treatment does not only benefit the patient and his family, but it also gives meaning and dignity to the medical team. It enriches their work experience. In an ideal case, the combined effort of lab technicians, doctors, nurses, and others helps carry the weight of the disease for the patient by reducing stress. The multidisciplinary team approach includes nutritionists, occupational therapists (OT), physical therapists (PT), and others. Grief counselors, social workers, and clergy can help with anxiety for both the patient and family. The team can also include hairstylists, make-up, fashion, and accessory stylists to mitigate the effects of body image changes. Can the exhausted, distraught, and often disoriented patient trust in the good intentions of the medical team?

In chronic conditions, many nonprofit social networks and social media sites such as the American Cancer Society and AARP, offer support, motivation, and encouragement. Support groups frequently improve treatment outcomes by promoting the understanding and handling of the disease. Their experience extends a window into the medical world and affords collective wisdom that turns the threat of the unknown into a manageable experience. During the progression of the disease, being open toward your medical staff, friends, and family, allows you to maintain a positive vision.

We are in the middle of a revolution. Promising treatments for chronic conditions are becoming available almost every day. New protocols and medications can enhance the efficacy of old remedies. Treatment options are increasingly based on personal comfort and genetic advantages. Such methods include pain control without the severe side effects that would interfere with normal activities of daily living. A better understanding of treatment options, as well as the variety of medicines, allows patients to become the managers of their care.

The Varied Effects of Stress

"If you don't think your anxiety, depression, sadness,
and stress impact your physical health, think again. All
of these emotions trigger chemical reactions in your
body, which can lead to inflammation and a weakened
immune system. Learn how to cope, sweet friend.
There will always be dark days."

—KRIS CARR

We are the first generation to analyze scientifically how our feelings influence our behavior. Stress has become a perennial problem of our time; it occurs across the social spectrum and in all age groups. It can even affect children. Stress forms when added expectations, particularly under unfamiliar conditions or adverse circumstances, inhibit timely information processing. Stress can be either a trigger or an aggravating factor for many diseases and pathologies. The rigidity and harshness of the sterile hospital environment can lead to confusion and fear; this added stressor can exacerbate the condition.

Although stress affects everybody at one time or another, the same stressors influence people very differently. The discriminative nature and apparent specificity of mental tension highlight its subjective nature: a link to self-confidence, and your belief in your *Self*. Although it often remains hidden from conscious awareness, stress causes insecurity and impatience. It weakens motivation, which handicaps productivity and performance. Anxiously clinging to situations, people, and God can interfere with brain functions, such as short-term memory. Over time, stress can lead to psychiatric symptoms. It can cause high blood pressure, heart attack, stroke, and weakened immune system.

Managing Stress

Because stress can contribute to personal growth, its elimination is neither practical nor prudent. Tension protects us from harm by heightening our senses. The danger lies in log-term anxiety. You should focus on getting rid of chronic stress by better management of time, resources, and interpersonal relationships. Every time you can handle your challenges, it increases your confidence. A belief in a Higher Power lends trust to better manage problems and negative emotional states. Prayer can lead to a sense of meaning, purpose, and self-transcendence.

Constant medical engagements lead to information overload. It strains focus and fractures attention and does not leave any downtime for relaxation and reflection. Physical exhaustion (exercise) can refresh the mind, but mental fatigue (such as dealing with the disease) exhausts the spirit and the body as well. Is there a light in the darkness? Practices introduced in the next station can help to achieve positive change through acceptance.

PROLOGUE OF THE EARTHLY PARADISE (1–4)

Of Heaven or Hell I have no power to sing,
I cannot ease the burden of your fears,
Or make quick-coming death a little thing,
Or bring again the pleasure of past years,
Nor for my words shall ye forget your tears,
Or hope again for aught that I can say,
The idle singer of an empty day.

But rather, when aweary of your mirth,
From full hearts still unsatisfied ye sigh,
And, feeling kindly unto all the earth,
Grudge every minute as it passes by,
Made the more mindful that the sweet days die—
—Remember me a little then I pray,
The idle singer of an empty day.

The heavy trouble, the bewildering care
That weighs us down who live and earn our bread,
These idle verses have no power to bear;
So let me sing of names remembered,
Because they, living not, can ne'er be dead,
Or long time take their memory quite away
From us poor singers of an empty day.

Dreamer of dreams, born out of my due time,
Why should I strive to set the crooked straight?
Let it suffice me that my murmuring rhyme
Beats with light wing against the ivory gate,
Telling a tale not too importunate
To those who in the sleepy region stay,
Lulled by the singer of an empty day.
        By William Morris

STATION VI

Veronica Wipes the Face of Jesus

"The spirit of a man will sustain his infirmity; but a
wounded spirit who can bear?"

—Proverbs 18:14 (ASV)

6, COMFORTED BY STRANGERS

"I lay me down and slept,
I awaked for the Lord sustained me."

—PSALM 3: 5 (KJB)

"I will be a Father to you and you will be my sons and
daughters, says the Lord Almighty."

—CORINTHIANS 6:18 (NIV)

"I now know how to plan my life and direct my path
because God is doing this for me by doing it through me."

—ERNEST HOLMES

Veronica is a mystery woman who is not mentioned among Jesus' followers. Unlike Simon, she risks her safety to comfort Jesus with dampened white linen. By wiping Jesus' face, the courageous, compassionate woman performs a simple, pious act. As we imagine her administering to the beaten, dust-covered Jesus, time appears to stand still. Veronica's action highlights the moral support of unforeseen charity received from strangers. During challenging times, the experience of help, kindness, or goodwill can boost our moral strength and restore our dignity. It can be proof of normalcy.

Senator John McCain was a prisoner of war during the Vietnam War. Held in solitary confinement, he was regularly interrogated by his captors. Despite the strict rule that forbade any communication, the detainees tried to contact each other by using signals, such as Morse code. When McCain was caught talking this way with a fellow inmate, he was punished severely. They wrapped his body tightly in ropes to restrict his movements and his circulation overnight. As he lay in painful confinement, a young guard entered his cell and motioned for him to remain silent as he relaxed his restraints. Only at dawn, before his actions could be discovered, did he restore the tight hold around his body.

The common bond between McCain and his guard became apparent a few months later, on a chilly Christmas morning. The guard stood close to his prisoner and drew a cross with his foot in the sand. Neither of the men had to say a word or look at each other. The simple gesture in the dirt formed a sacred communion. The guard rubbed out his marking before he walked away. Thus lays the power of kindness, even in a prison camp. In an appreciated, dignified, and meaningful moment, we can touch each other's souls.

The experience was more meaningful because of the miserable conditions the men shared. Moments that feed the soul are noticed and appreciated more in trying times, which allows people to gather strength from them. As the brain replays these moments, they are understood and treasured better; small details are noticed and given meaning. In loneliness, such meaningful moments can become guiding beacons and the source of moral and physical strength. The same can happen in a hospital room, where the patient is both closed in and reliant on others. Dependence can degrade the patient into a helpless, infantile condition. The hospital staff is paid to serve the patient, but a smile, a straightened pillow, or a cheery hello gives the patient a reason to hope again and feel valued. As previously mentioned, support groups also fill that role.

Our need for human closeness is formidable. We long for someone to touch us in the depth of our soul. Many use cynicism and disdain to cover up vulnerability and emotional hunger. How can we recognize and appreciate personal closeness? Cultivating our spirituality enhances our ability to treasure special moments of life. Spirituality is a special appreciation for creation.

Cultivating Your Spirituality

"Feelings come and go like clouds in a windy sky.
Conscious breathing is my anchor."

—THICH NHAT HAHN[3]

3. Nhat Hanh, *Stepping into Freedom: An Introduction to Buddhist Monastic Training*, 8.

"To understand the immeasurable, the mind must be
extraordinarily quiet, still."

—JIDDU KRISHNAMURTI

"Nature does not hurry, yet everything is
accomplished."

—LAO TZU

Spirituality has a more inclusive meaning than just being religious; it includes those who do not believe in a higher power but still search for purpose in something bigger than themselves. Focusing on the sacred or transcendent is an appreciation of all humanity and even nature. Therefore, spirituality is at the heart of every major religion. Without spirituality, religion is like a boat without a rudder. The following spiritual practices help you to develop your sense of aliveness and interconnectedness with all of Creation.

1. Negative emotions enslave us with repetitive thought patterns that lead to separation and anxiety. Positive expressions, such as "rejoice" and "being glad," are expressions recurring with high frequency in the Scripture. We must take this to heart and seek happiness for ourselves, for our friends and family. Celebrate God's creation every day by expanding your personal world with joy and love.

2. Enhance mental flexibility: Mental flexibility is the ability to remain congruent with the flow of things. It is the motivation to adapt to change, whatever those changes might bring. Modern science tells us that social connections and trust in our environment permits better outcomes in disease conditions. In the Gospels, Matthew 5:16 (NIV) we read, "let your light shine before others, that they may see your good deeds and glorify your Father in heaven." The courage to carry on despite danger overcomes fear and the risk of failure. It is the willingness to plan for tomorrow when the disease might take that tomorrow away.

3. Meditation and Yoga practice: Meditation is a prime example of controlling one's thoughts to create emotional neutrality and equanimity. Eastern religious practitioners and sages have explored and perfected various practices that guide attention toward the experience of the present moment. The methods relieve residual energies of self-centered, stressful states, and enhance the emotional stability of the inner world, thoughts, feelings, and self-talk. Regular meditation increases satisfaction, happiness, and joy.

The type of meditation you chose should be appropriate for your personality, life situation, and the specific problem(s) you are facing (several examples are listed below). Meditation deflects focus from past issues or from the anxiety of the future. Ignoring the past and the future focuses the mind within the moment, from which events can naturally unfold. External observation of your biological reactions creates a broader perspective, which promotes liberation and independence. Stepping out of the egoistic internal viewpoint purges the soul from the accumulated information overload, replacing it with meaning. *The awareness of your emotional state is immensely empowering.* Because emotions underlie thoughts and behavior, changing them can gradually reprogram your life.

Breathing Practices

Breathing, an integral part of yoga practice and meditation, can relax and detoxify the body. Yoga is an Eastern spiritual practice that aims to create a sense of inner union through physical postures and proper breathing. The in and out rhythm of breath is a very familiar activity, which can become meditative, calming, and relaxing. Conscious breathing sends impulses from the cortex, which has an impact on emotions. Focusing on resentments and negativity while you exhale releases tension. Mindful breathing can elevate and evolve your mind. This simple exercise can make you feel powerful and confident, making problems appear less significant. Systematic yoga practice can reduce depression, stress, and anxiety; it lowers blood pressure and inflammation in the body and increases wellbeing.

Relaxing Your Body

Lie down or sit in a comfortable position on a chair, bed, or a rug. Close your eyes, and make sure you will not be disturbed for a while. Have soothing music on, and soft light, if you like. Think about your body parts starting with your feet and relax each in turn. If your body is still tense, concentrate your focus on that specific body part. Repeat the practice until you can remain relaxed from disturbing thoughts. Enjoy your newfound freedom.

Quote Meditation

We are persons of our beliefs. Although our life changes continuously with our circumstances, our confidence rests in the solidity and stability of our positions. As our convictions change, outdated opinions can cause inner turmoil, suffering, and depression. Therefore, it is necessary to adapt to the times. It is not enough to talk about acceptance; you must internalize the new truth in your mind. The changes to the brain's wiring produce positive transformations in hormonal and immune function and healing.

A quote distills a complex problem into its essential nugget and points toward a resolution with the authority of truth. Quotes can mend and update your conflicted mindset. Actively collect quotes; collect ones that speak to you and relate to your present situation. The Bible is full of wisdom, and the internet is an endless resource.

In your mind, the two thoughts (the quote and your own), like a see-saw, compete for dominance. Your task is to replace your misconceptions with a new understanding. The practice gradually modifies the connections in the brain to formulate the insight and wisdom of your chosen quote. Internalizing the new belief automatically and instantaneously abandons the old mental state.

You may attain a higher perspective in as soon as an hour. Significant mental changes may require regular practice for weeks or even months. Nevertheless, the weakening of the static and stressful mental patterns allows positive effects to take root much sooner. Similar benefits can be achieved by learning a musical piece, foreign language, or even the practice of arts and crafts. Picking a task just above your mastery will challenge your mental focus.

The practice can powerfully replace old, outdated beliefs with new ones. It will give you strength; it will improve your understanding of yourself and provide you with the power to adapt to change. It will turn you from a victim to a victor.

TWO KINDS OF PEOPLE

There are two kinds of people on earth to-day;
Just two kinds of people, no more I say.

Not the sinner and saint, for it's well understood
The good are half bad and the bad are half good.

Not the rich and the poor, for to rate a man's wealth,
You must first know the state of his conscience and health.

Not the humble and proud, for in life's little span,
Who puts on vain airs, is not counted a man.

Not the happy and sad, for the swift flying years
Bring each man his laughter end each man his tears.

No; the two kinds of people on earth I mean
Are the people who lift and the people who lean.

Wherever you go you will find the earth's masses
Are always divided in just these two classes.

And oddly enough, you will find, too, I ween,
There's only one lifter to twenty who lean.

In which class are you? Are you easing the load
Of overtaxed lifters who toil down the road?

Or are you a leaner who lets others bear
Your portion of labor and worry and care?

    By Ella Wheeler Wilcox.

STATION VII

Jesus Falls the Second Time

"Be merciful to me, O God, be merciful to me! For my
soul trusts in You; And in the shadow of Your wings
I will make my refuge, Until *these* calamities have
passed by."

—Psalm 57:1 (NKJV)

7, STRUGGLING WITH THE DISEASE

"My grace is sufficient for you,
for my power is made perfect in weakness."

—2 CORINTHIAN, 12:9 (NIV)

"For as the heaven is high above the earth, so great is
his mercy toward them that fear him."

—PSALM 103:11 (KJB)

"Trust in the LORD. Have faith, do not despair.
Trust in the LORD."

—PSALM 27:14 (GNT)

Jesus falls again. Although no longer carrying the Cross, his condition worsens on the long trek up the hill to Golgotha. Jesus is not exempt from intense suffering. The loss of blood from the scourging made him weak and dehydrated, and increasingly delirious. Christ is our brother in our struggle, injury, and death.

"So do not worry, saying, 'What shall we eat?' or 'What shall we drink?' or 'What shall we wear?' For the pagans run after all these things, and your heavenly Father knows that you need them. But seek first his kingdom and his righteousness, and all these things will be given to you as well," Matthew: 6:31–33 (NIV).

The loss of control over the outcome, such as negative test results, or a plateau in your treatment can lead to desperation. The passing of fellow patients turns thoughts toward dying. Damages in dignity and self-respect challenge the sense of normalcy. We are reminded of Matthew: 6:34 (NLT), "So don't worry about tomorrow, for tomorrow will bring its own worries. Today's trouble is enough for today."

Seneca expresses a similar thought: "There are more things likely to frighten us than there are to crush us; we suffer more often in imagination than in reality." By focusing on the things within our power, we create a "healing environment." Paying attention to the little things can make a big difference in the outcome. Alternative therapies can aid in better management of the disease and your psychology. Smaller meal portions or easy exercises can help transition you through the treatments. Discussing your changing experiences with your medical team, physicians, psychologists, physical therapists, nutritionists, and others help to monitor your condition. Even choosing appropriate makeup or wigs can make a big difference in your sense of self.

All over the world, Christmas celebrations remember Jesus' simple birth. The pine tree, a regular part of the holiday decoration, is the sign of everlasting life with God. My first Christmas tree was a young pine. My father bought it with roots, so he could plant it in our garden to commemorate my birth. The seedling quickly grew to be a slender, healthy tree among the fruit trees in our orchard.

I was 16 when a poor soul snuck into our garden to cut down the top of my tree for his Christmas celebration. My wounded tree grew two side by side trunks, but the green branches still tried to conquer the sky. The disease can steal the hope for the future for patients who are handicapped or facing an infirm existence. Severely injured or paralyzed soldiers and people often contemplate suicide. Changes in body image, side effects of the treatment, pain, and lack of treatment progression can combine into a sense of paralyzing brokenness. Just like the pine tree, you can always form a new future. It might be very different from the one you imagined when you were young, healthy, and whole, but your goal should still be to conquer the entire sky.

When we notice that we are driving our car in the wrong direction, we take the nearest exit and study the map. This is true in life too. When you repeatedly find yourself disappointed in your treatment option, then it is time to reexamine your decision or reevaluate your goals. People who follow a path for a long time often do not risk changing direction. They do not want to waste all their work, effort, and time or disappoint others. By continuing life unchanged, they get further and further down the wrong path.

You have to be able to admit to yourself when you fail. The experience of failure can lead you towards a better path. A correction to align with your goal will give you more appreciation for it than if you achieved it for the first time. The most frequent obstructions to rational decision making are pain and depression. We will discuss them in subsequent sections.

Pain

"Sit with the pain until it passes, and you will be
calmer for the next one."

—NAVAL RAVIKANT

Pain, a significant symptom in many medical conditions, has a varied and vital repertoire in conscious function and self-preservation. At its most basic form, hurt is a persuasive argument about potential harm and urges one to escape. For example, it can cause you to avoid particular body positions or situations. Ironically though, pain can be associated with positive feelings, such as muscle soreness after a good physical workout or aches after a successful medical treatment (physical therapy). Therefore, suffering, which includes mental distress, is an indicator of your mental state. Your pain tolerance closely reflects your stress level and satisfaction.

The modern understanding recognizes pain as a subjective experience, which inspired a paradigm shift toward natural treatments. For example, diverting attention from pain through motivation, musical stimulation, and art activities can improve pain tolerance. Similar results are found with yoga, exercise, and psychological interventions, such as hypnosis and cognitive behavioral therapy. Looking at pictures of romantic partners, or even thinking about them can improve your pain tolerance.

Revisiting depressive periods by sharing the experiences in group therapy, can ease mental distress and inspire meaning and resilience. In extreme cases, the automatic urge to re-live pain repeatedly perpetuates the mental anguish and suffering, a condition called post-traumatic stress disorder or PTSD. Novel, noninvasive techniques, such as HIRREM (high-resolution, relational, reso-nance-based, electro encephalic mirroring), might help sufferers.

Observing the physiological manifestations of your own pain experience can significantly lessen its subjective bite. For this rea-son, the most important words a patient needs to hear is "the pain will go away soon." The faith that our emotional pains are also tem-porary provides similar mental liberation.

Depression

"I could disappear forever and it wouldn't make any difference."

—Anonymous

Occasional stress is a normal part of a confident and resilient life. The initial struggles of the illness usually do not trigger depression because spiritual well-being protects us. However, the insecurity of repeated failures and setbacks of the disease forces mood swings, and mental/emotional degradation, which wear down mental resil-ience. Mental exhaustion and enervation increase the vulnerability for depression. Without motivation and enthusiasm, the image of the future disappears, and life is lived on a day-to-day basis, lim-ited to basic survival. Chronic pain is particularly dangerous; it can compromise spiritual energies, inspiration, and joy. Existing stereotypes about chronic disease also negatively influence one's psychology.

In chronic diseases, depression is more difficult to recognize, diagnose, and manage. Some disorders (particularly neurologic syndromes such as stroke or Parkinson's) do affect brain chemistry, causing depression-like symptoms. Depression sucks away mental energy reserves and reduces pain tolerance. It steals the will toward social and personal engagement. The deficient functionality handi-caps psychological orientation and the capacity for interaction. In a mentally and physically exhausted state, even solving everyday problems becomes challenging. Difficulties with sleep, eating, energy, concentration, or self-image reduce the effectiveness of treatment. Under the psychological heaviness of the disease, it is almost impossible not to consider one's mortality. When we are down, it is hard to look up to see the light.

Treatment and Prevention

"There are far, far better things ahead
than anything we leave behind."

—C.S. Lewis[4]

One of the early symptoms of depression is a strong, almost irresistible pull toward isolation. The most effective preventative self-help measure is the close embrace of family and friends. Robust social support networks buffer stress, pain, depression, and anxiety. Immersing yourself with trust in your social circle will miraculously bring you the help you need and strengthen your spirit. Patients having trusted friendships report higher levels of happiness, better disease outcomes, and lower mortality rates.

Because depression hinders recall of positive memories, creating and reactivating rewarding experiences can be a natural remedy. Reconnecting with fallen out friends or long-lost relatives even from afar can boost wellbeing. Self-management of treatment choices, in conjunction with the medical team, also fortifies resistance to depression.

Optimal sleep increases the quality of life, enhancing intelligence, bodily function, and emotional stability. It can spur a fresh perspective. Arts, music, and natural beauty improve mental flexibility, and humor is an instant confidence booster. Rest boosts the body's internal resources, easing stress. Attending a concert, viewing art in a gallery, walking in nature or a park, or reading thoughtful lines in a book can provide a short mental vacation.

In our fast-paced world, handicrafts and manual work are viewed as old-fashioned. Nevertheless, these activities cultivate a

4. Lewis, *Letter to Mary Willis Shelburne.*

sense of beauty, balance, and joy. Even in trauma, their inspiring, meditative actions improve mood. The slow, steady progress from our own two hands generates confidence and inner growth. Art-making can improve resilience toward stress and depression. The creation of beauty in arts, music, and crafts (knitting, music-making, and cooking) encourages positive social interactions. Sharing resources and your creations forms a better community. Reaching for small goals keeps the mind open and engaged, inspiring satisfaction and happiness and reducing pain and depression. All of these things are important but no less important is seeking out some form of psychotherapy. Being comfortable with your therapist is crucial. You can choose either group or individual format, local or internet-based treatment options. Meaning-Centered therapy focuses on meaning and spiritual well-being. It helps to preserve and recover personal values and reduce the negative impact of the disease.

Jesus' faith in his almighty father helped him cope with his ordeal. "For we live by faith, not by sight," says Corinthians 5:7 (NIV). Similarly, in Hebrews 11:1, "The assurance of things hoped for, the conviction of things not seen." The repetitive ordering of life through prayer cultivates a religious self and promotes a better handling of the disease. "Now to him who is able to do immeasurably more than all we ask or imagine, according to his power that is at work within us." Ephesians 3:20 (NIV)

MY LIFE HAD STOOD—A LOADED GUN (764)

My Life had stood—a Loaded Gun -
In Corners—till a Day
The Owner passed—identified -
And carried Me away -

And now We roam in Sovreign Woods -
And now We hunt the Doe -
And every time I speak for Him
The Mountains straight reply -

And do I smile, such cordial light
Opon the Valley glow -
It is as a Vesuvian face
Had let it's pleasure through -

And when at Night—Our good Day done -
I guard My Master's Head -
'Tis better than the Eider Duck's
Deep Pillow—to have shared -

To foe of His—I'm deadly foe -
None stir the second time -
On whom I lay a Yellow Eye -
Or an emphatic Thumb -

Though I than He—may longer live
He longer must—than I -
For I have but the power to kill,
Without—the power to die –
    By Emily Dickinson

STATION VIII

Jesus Meets the Women of Jerusalem

"Be strong and courageous. Do not be afraid or terrified because of them, for the Lord your God goes with you; he will never leave you nor forsake you."

—DEUTERONOMY 31:6 (NIV)

8, SOCIAL CONNECTIONS

"How can the guests of the bridegroom mourn while he is with them? The time will come when the bridegroom will be taken from them; then they will fast."

—Matthew: 9:15–17 (NIV)

"But those who wait on the LORD
Shall renew *their* strength;
They shall mount up with wings like eagles,
They shall run and not be weary,
They shall walk and not faint."

—Isaiah 40:31 (NKJV)

Jesus' followers, who expected him to bring forth an Earthly Kingdom, witness the humiliation and torture of their rabbi instead. Despite the prospect of his death, Jesus turns his sympathizing attention to his followers. He consoles the distraught women and eases their abandonment and disorientation.

Those who are helping others shift their focus away from the disease, which releases stress and anxiety. Animal studies have shown that grooming behavior enhances resistance against disease. When patients console their families, friends, and others, they have a lower concentration of inflammatory markers, which improves their chances of recovery. Heart patients, who counsel others, have significantly better parameters of blood pressure and recovery time. The generosity of attention has been dubbed "Helpers High" because of its ability to improve immune function and disease outcomes.

Antoine de Saint-Exupery's book, *The Little Prince*, describes the friendship between the lonely little prince and a shy fox. Their trust in each other enhances their lives independent of their situation, appearances, or social status. The fox's words: "One sees clearly only with the heart" exemplifies the depth and power of social connectedness.

Joining a cancer support group provides access to resources and community support. People who went before you on the dark journey of the disease can supply you with a treasure trove of experience not available for anyone else. Journaling can be an alternative to people with reserved personalities, who do not feel comfortable openly expressing themselves. Writing an autobiographical story, poetry, or sharing the disease experience in some other way is a great way to gain meaning, and it provides others with helpful information.

Having family members present during doctor's visits eases the burden. I was fortunate enough to be able to accompany my mother for her cancer treatments. During outpatient treatments, she could keep her street clothes and footwear on, giving her a sense of homeyness in the sterile surroundings. The latter was especially a blessing with her swollen ankles. On days, when the treatment room was occupied, she could stay in an empty patient room. On one occasion, hooked up to chemotherapy, she was reclining comfortably with her well-trusted Birkenstocks on the white linens. A new patient, who just arrived to occupy the second bed, gave her stern reminders about the rudeness of wearing shoes in bed. My mother, however, remained stoic and calm. The absence of the expected reprisal or even acknowledgment only fueled the woman's ire. She kept up the barrage of nasty comments until the end of the procedure.

My mother had severe hearing loss. She mostly relied on lip-reading rather than a hearing aid. Enclosed in her thoughts, she probably did not even notice the woman coming into the room. Her handicap ultimately spared her from the woman's chastising. When her session was finished, my mother got out of bed and very kindly said goodbye to her temporary roommate. The woman was utterly flabbergasted to find that her verbal attacks had no effect! Embarrassed and regretful, she said goodbye to my mother with kindness and respect.

Although my mother's decency originated in ignorance, her story is a testament to the power of kindness. People and animals naturally gravitate toward those who make them feel better. Just like the sun, which supports life, the positive energy of love inspires trust, harmony, and peace in the world. Independent of your circumstances, your inner light warms the hearts of others and betters the world. Although you will not make friends with everybody, making an attempt to better your relationships goes a long way.

Lack of trust indicates insecurity, which is corrosive to relationships and the self. Negativity, anger, and suspicion push people away and impede healing. If seeds perish one year from frost or lack of rain, the farmer will still trust the land and the environment to grow a new crop the following spring. In literature and film, the essential nature of belief made it possible for the Wizard of Oz to give out certificates of courage to the lion, heart to the tin man, and brain to the scarecrow. For the characters in the Wizard of Oz, trust in the system made all the difference; likewise, belief in the medical team and procedure is an essential part of healing. Many examples from the Gospel emphasize trust. Although Peter follows Jesus, his attempt to walk on water fails due to his lack of confidence. Touching Jesus' cloak healed an unnamed woman from her bleeding (Matthew 9:20–22, Mark 5:25–34, Luke 8:43–48). Her healing occurs through faith. The role of belief probably is never more evident than in Matthew 21:22 (NIV), "If you believe, you will receive whatever you ask for in prayer."

Trust in Your Closeness to God

"The LORD is close to the brokenhearted and saves
those who are crushed in spirit."

—PSALM 34:18 (NIV)

"Draw near to God, and he will draw near to you."

—JAMES 4:8 (ESV)

"The LORD is near to all who call on him, to all who
call on him in truth."

—PSALM 145:18 (NIV)

The rewards of trust are everywhere in the Bible. And today, science confirms the immense potential of faith. Trust is an emotion that cannot be obtained without fully paying its price first. Trust is earned. Experiencing support every day, systematically doing our best, forms a trust. Therefore the size of our belief and faith depends on the depth of our commitment. "But when you ask, you must believe and not doubt, because the one who doubts is like a wave of the sea, blown and tossed by the wind," James 1:6 (NIV). Again and again, the Gospels, such as Matthew 17:20, and Jeremiah 17:7, confirm the power of faith.

> But blessed is the one who trusts in the Lord,
> whose confidence is in him.
> They will be like a tree planted by the water
> that sends out its roots by the stream.
> It does not fear when heat comes;
> its leaves are always green.
> It has no worries in a year of drought
> and never fails to bear fruit.
> (Jeremiah 17:7–8 NIV)

> Commit your way to the Lord;
> trust in him and he will do this:
> He will make your righteous reward shine like the dawn,
> your vindication like the noonday sun.
> (Psalm 37:5–6 NIV)

Form Love

> "I trust your love, and I feel like celebrating
> because you rescued me."
>
> —Psalm 13:5 (CEV)

Love is the most potent and most important form of trust. It is the most authentic way to form a unity with God. All major religions emphasize a connection to others by altruistic love. True love is an immeasurable gift that can achieve any goal and accomplish any task. In every civilization, there are stories of the power of love, which transforms and motivates achievement. Compassion, love, and kindness promote healing and the state of wellbeing.

The expression of love, both earthly and Godly, are abound in the Bible. Corinthians 13:4–8 (NIV) is particularly beautiful: "Love is patient, love is kind. It does not envy; it does not boast, it is not proud. It does not dishonor others, it is not self-seeking, it is not easily angered, it keeps no record of wrongs. Love does not delight in evil but rejoices with the truth. It always protects, always trusts, always hope, always perseveres. Love never fails."

Love seems to be one of the main messages of the Bible. We find in 1 John 4:16 (NIV) "And so we know and rely on the love God has for us. God is love. Whoever lives in love lives in God, and God in them."

PRAYER OF SAINT FRANCIS OF ASSISI

Lord, make me an instrument of your peace.
Where there is hatred, let me bring love.
Where there is offense, let me bring pardon.
Where there is discord, let me bring union.
Where there is error, let me bring truth.
Where there is doubt, let me bring faith.
Where there is despair, let me bring hope.
Where there is darkness, let me bring your light.
Where there is sadness, let me bring joy.
O Master, let me not seek as much
to be consoled as to console,
to be understood as to understand,
to be loved as to love,
for it is in giving that one receives,
it is in self-forgetting that one finds,
it is in pardoning that one is pardoned,
it is in dying that one is raised to eternal life.

LOVE IS STRENGTH

Love alone is great in might,
Makes the heavy burden light,
Smooths rough ways to weary feet,
Makes the bitter morsel sweet:
Love alone is strength!

Might that is not born of Love
Is not Might born from above,
Has its birthplace down below
Where they neither reap nor sow:
Love alone is strength!

Love is stronger than all force,
Is its own eternal source;
Might is always in decay,
Love grows fresher every day:
Love alone is strength!

Little ones, no ill can chance;
Fear ye not, but sing and dance;
Though the high-heaved heaven should fall
God is plenty for us all:
God is Love and Strength!
  By George MacDonald

STATION IX

Jesus Falls for the Third Time

"Reproach hath broken my heart; and I am full of
heaviness: And I looked for some to take pity, but there
was none; and for comforters, but I found none."

—Psalms 69:20 (KJB)

9, GIVING UP CONTROL

"My heart is smitten, and whithered like grass; so that I
forget to eat my bread."

—PSALM 102:4 (KJB)

"Pain is important: how we evade it, how we succumb
to it, how we deal with it, how we transcend it."

—AUDRE LORDE

"We cannot live fully without becoming aware of the
fragility and finiteness of life."

—IRVIN D. YALOM[5]

We see the humanity of Jesus again and again on his journey to
Golgotha. His weakness, his need for assistance, his willingness to
sympathize with others, and his final submission to death, all testify
to his identity as Human. His vulnerability permits us to relate to
him during the changing course of the illness. Jesus' acceptance of
his condition points beyond here and now. The initial desperation
and fight for life are replaced by the acceptance of death. Accepting
the will of God can empower you during this difficult and trying
period. The little joys of life, such as listening to calming music or
enjoying art while lying in bed, can give a sense of normalcy. Often,
the inevitability of death helps us appreciate and have immense
gratitude for the value of life.

The so-called "fight or flight" response provokes primal
physical reactions, such as sweating, increased heart rate, and high
adrenaline levels in the blood. In some cases, anger can spur constructive change, but fear is the avoidance of all kinds of action.
There is no escape from the hole of helplessness, which is fear. The
paralyzing, overwhelming emotion prevents constructive reason-
ing and thinking, and causes failure. Without the ability to think, to

5. Yalom, *Curing the Dread of Death: Theory, Research and Practice*, 187.

plan, or to act, our capacity for renewal and wisdom is diminished. Immobility, indecision, and helplessness inhibit reasoned decision making. "Fear makes the wolf bigger than he is," says the German proverb. Fear shoots down every opportunity for help. Because negative emotions can also be incapacitating, they show a close relationship to fear.

Overcoming the Fear of Death

"When you're facing death, you have to walk that walk alone."

—VIV ALBERTINE[6]

Death is simple for the very strong and those who are weakened by the loss of all hope. Heroes and wise men or women know that death does not defeat them. Like the wind and the sunshine, their spirit lives on. Strength lends optimism and equanimity even to passing. No matter how fiercely you protest death, eventually, you must arrive at its door. In the long struggle, you might lose the loving touch of your loved ones and miss the possibility to change the course of your disease. The tension robs you of wisdom, relationships, and intimacy with God. You cannot enjoy the precious last weeks, months, or years of life.

Fear is an impending sense of danger. The thoughts of vulnerability trigger a constant and futile search to safeguard against instability. The energy that you invest in assurances remains just a temporary fix. Like a mirage, safety always remains out of reach for an insecure person. The sense of security comes from within.

Presenting your story as a failure and a hopeless case will manifest itself as a disappointment in real life. Even the perceived difficulty of a task is a fear that can instigate procrastination by manufacturing artificial business, excuses, or complete blockage or exclusion of a subject matter. As jumping into cold water cures

6. Albertine, *Clothes, Clothes, Clothes. Music, Music, Music. Boys, Boys, Boys.: A Memoir*, 296.

timidity, the most effective way to eliminate fear is to start with the management of the impending crisis head-on. Whenever anxiety influences your decisions, act! Action, even a small one, pierces the paralyzing tightness by diminishing the automatic fear-response. Meeting it head-on is an intimidating and often nervous, but profoundly empowering, first step. Defeating anxiety in this way boosts confidence. The exercise will increase your resistance to fear, even the foreboding of death.

How to accept the peace of death? You can visualize your life as a computer simulation. In this virtual reality, nobody can hurt you. This profoundly empowering exercise can help reduce your fear. When you have progressed toward managing your anxiety this way, you have moved toward accepting that you are going to die. The ability to imagine your own passing can eliminate its fear from your soul.

When we embrace death, it loses its power. Accommodating to passing infuses your actions with fearlessness, which is perceived by others as wisdom. Accepting that you are going to die is the fastest way to free your courage. Conceding to his imminent death by ALS (a motor neuron disease) in his twenties, the physicist Stephen Hawking fortified his determination to make a difference in the world by his work.

We stay alive due to the trust we have in the food we eat and the water we drink. It provides us our survival and wellbeing. We trust that cars stop at the red light and allow others to pass. Without having faith in others, the system, we become stiff, tense, and suspicious. A suffering mind prepares for danger by putting up protective walls. And this is a very tiresome, exhausting way to live. When you accept your final peace, your heart will open; then, you will notice how the sunshine plays on spring leaves, the beauty of people, and the world. Your open heart gives you an appreciation for the joy and happiness you see in others, and it will be reflected back.

You are alive today for a reason. All the hopelessness of the future cannot erase the experiences and riches of your life, a life well-lived. The ability to rest between the pains, see the smile of a caregiver and hope for tomorrow are gifts of this special day. Gratitude heals the soul and can point it toward the final acceptance of death. With God's graciousness, our soul is now prepared for its ultimate home.

> A human being is a part of the whole called by us 'the universe'—a part limited in time and space. He experiences himself, his thoughts and feelings, as something separate from the rest—a kind of optical delusion of consciousness. This delusion is a kind of prison for us, restricting us to our personal desires and affection for a few persons nearest to us. Our task must be to free ourselves from this prison by widening the circle of understanding and compassion to embrace all living creatures and the whole of nature in its beauty. (Albert Einstein)

Our existence on Earth is limited in space and time. We have to exchange our temporary material state for an eternal presence in heaven.

UP-HILL

Does the road wind up-hill all the way?
    Yes, to the very end.
Will the day's journey take the whole long day?
    From morn to night, my friend.

But is there for the night a resting-place?
    A roof for when the slow dark hours begin.
May not the darkness hide it from my face?
    You cannot miss that inn.

Shall I meet other wayfarers at night?
    Those who have gone before.
Then must I knock, or call when just in sight?
    They will not keep you standing at that door.

Shall I find comfort, travel-sore and weak?
    Of labour you shall find the sum.
Will there be beds for me and all who seek?
    Yea, beds for all who come.
    By Christina Rossetti

SOLITUDE

Laugh, and the world laughs with you;
    Weep, and you weep alone;
For the sad old earth must borrow its mirth,
    But has trouble enough of its own.
Sing, and the hills will answer;
    Sigh, it is lost on the air;
The echoes bound to a joyful sound,
    But shrink from voicing care.

Rejoice, and men will seek you;
    Grieve, and they turn and go;
They want full measure of all your pleasure,
    But they do not need your woe.
Be glad, and your friends are many;
    Be sad, and you lose them all,
There are none to decline your nectared wine,
    But alone you must drink life's gall.

Feast, and your halls are crowded;
    Fast, and the world goes by.
Succeed and give, and it helps you live,
    But no man can help you die.
There is room in the halls of pleasure
    For a large and lordly train,
But one by one we must all file on
    Through the narrow aisles of pain.
    By Ella Wheeler Wilcox

STATION X

Jesus Is Stripped of His Garments

"They part my garments among them and cast lots
upon my vesture."

—Psalms 22:18 (KJV)

10, GIVING UP POSSESSIONS

"I am weary of my crying: my throat is dried: mine
eyes fail while I wait for my God."

—PSALM 69.3 (NIV)

"The night kissed the fading day
With a whisper.
I am death, your mother,
From me you will get new birth."

—RABINDRANATH TAGORE

The humiliation of Jesus is complete in the loss of his garments. There is a meditative quietness about this passage. The clothes are a metaphor for earthly possessions, and giving up anything and everything at this stage is easy. In St. Paul's words, Jesus "emptied himself," by divesting himself of everything, even his meager earthly belongings. The soldiers cast lots to divide the garments of the dying Jesus amongst themselves.

Jesus said, "Whoever wants to save their life will lose it, but whoever loses his life for me will find it," Matthew 16:25 (NIV). Likewise in Saint Augustine's City of God (Book XIV: 28): "Two cities have been formed by two loves: the earthly by the love of self, even to the contempt of God; the heavenly by the love of God, even to the contempt of self." A similar idea is expressed in Matthew: 10:37–38 (NIV). Unhealthy attachments are a sign of insecurity. Conditional relationships with loved ones (fathers, mothers, sons, and daughters) are driven by self-doubt. True love does not deny liberty to those we cherish, it is unconditional. It shows confidence and generosity to all and malice to none.

Your impending death is a test of your faith. Not by sacrificing your loved ones (as in the case of Abraham) but by the peaceful acceptance of your passing. Abraham's willingness to sacrifice his only son was possible because of his faith and confidence in God. God's promise to Abraham for his sacrifice was abundant descendants.

Jesus's promise is even more awesome, "Very truly I tell you, whoever believes in me will do the work I have been doing, and they will do even greater things than these," John 14:12 (NIV).

The nineteen-century Indian saint, Vivekananda, says, "In the springtime observe the blossoms on the fruit trees, the blossoms vanish of themselves as the fruit grows. So too will the lower-self vanish as the divine grows within." Spiritual insight and redemption have the power to reclaim the past for happiness, satisfaction, and wisdom. The power of deliverance and divine blessing is present in the parable of the vineyard workers. Because every worker gets the same pay regardless of the length of service, devotion to God (whether you are Pope or pauper) is rewarded by the same salvation. "So the last will be first, and the first will be last," Matthew 20:16 (NIV), is an uplifting message of the gospels. Your personal redemption rests in your commitment.

In my childhood, I often stayed at my grandparents' farm. One day, I found their two dogs barking ferociously. It was getting dark; it was hard to see the dark spot about the size of a fist on the ground. It turned out to be a prickly ball of a hedgehog. The dogs could not challenge the animal, so they were barking at it from a distance. I curiously lifted it and cradled its thorny body in my palms; I felt its warmth. Tickling my hands, it slowly opened itself up just a little, so I could see its sharp, pink nose, hiding behind its armor. Your past is like that prickly hedgehog. When you are barking at it from a distance, it looks thorny, ugly, even menacing. But if you lift it gently in your mind, and hold it long enough with peaceful attention, it will open up and reveal its soft side, the side where wisdom and even love resides. Behind the thorns of pains and suffering lies the softness of understanding and acceptance of your mortality.

For a terminally ill patient, commitment to God eliminates the agony of why. Accepting the mortal test can strengthen or re-kindle our faith; it can spare us from spiritual death as we sacrifice our earthly self and ready ourselves for salvation. Giving up selfish powers frees the soul for redemption and the promise of the kingdom of heaven. In chronic diseases, the physical, behavioral, and psychological journey towards passing often starts several months before death. During this time, some people appear more confident, even enlightened, because their faith sustains them. Those whose belief is challenged might be less approachable and withdrawn. Resignation erodes the will for mortal life. This relatively lucid stage permits the patient to take care of personal business, such as repairing relationships or saying a dignified goodbye to loved ones. Giving up control over the material world liberates a spiritual dimension. Interest in life and social connections, even within the immediate family, becomes overwhelming. The hospital sends the patient home or to hospice.

IN TENEBRIS

"Percussus sum sicut foenum, et aruit cor meum."—Ps. ci.

Wintertime nighs;
But my bereavement-pain
It cannot bring again:
Twice no one dies.

Flower-petals flee;
But, since it once hath been,
No more that severing scene
Can harrow me.

Birds faint in dread:
I shall not lose old strength
In the lone frost's black length:
Strength long since fled!

Leaves freeze to dun;
But friends can not turn cold
This season as of old
For him with none.

Tempests may scath;
But love can not make smart
Again this year his heart
Who no heart hath.

Black is night's cope;
But death will not appal
One who, past doubtings all,
Waits in unhope.

    By Thomas Hardy

STATION XI

Jesus Is Nailed to the Cross

"My mouth is dried up like a potsherd, and my tongue
sticks to the roof of my mouth; you lay me in the dust
of death."

—Psalm 22:15 (NIV)

11, PREPARATION FOR DEATH

"Dogs surround me, a pack of villains encircles me;
they pierce my hands and my feet."

—PSALM 22:16 (NIV)

"They put gall in my food and gave me vinegar for my
thirst."

—PSALM 69:21 (NIV)

"They brought Jesus to the place called Golgotha (which means 'the place of the skull'). Then they offered him wine mixed with myrrh, but he did not take it. And they crucified him. Dividing up his clothes, they cast lots to see what each would get," Mark 15:22-26 (NIV).

Jesus probably had only limited awareness of his surroundings at the time of his crucifixion. His words, "it is complete," indicate his acceptance of his fate. Yet, he has concern for his killers, "Forgive them, father, for they do not know what they are doing," Luke 23:34 (NIV). He promises one of the men being crucified with him, "you will be with me in paradise." Finally, he speaks to his mother: "Woman, behold your son!" and turning to John, the beloved disciple, "Behold, your mother!" John 19:26-27 (NIV). He brings closure and comfort to everyone present and joins the fate of his mother and John, the people closest to him. He highlights once more the need to love and care for others, "Love one another. As I have loved you, so you must love one another." John 13:34.

Jesus forgave those who sinned against him. Forgiveness is essential to turn our human existence into a humane one. Desmond Tutu, Nobel Prize winner and chair of the Reconciliation Commission in South Africa, considers forgiveness a grace that allows victims to move forward to a better future. Both Ronald Reagan and John Paul the Second forgave the person who tried to kill them, as Jesus forgave his killers. Only forgiveness allows our soul to move beyond the negative energy of suffering. We should emulate Jesus' final act of mercy and forgive our enemies.

For believers, the irreversible barrier of death contains the promise of an afterlife. Agnostics and even atheists, when facing death, often experience a spiritual and religious awakening. The medical treatments are exhausted, and God remains. Planning one's funeral and remembrances via video or audio recordings might help to achieve peace and closure for loved ones and our final confirmation. Social media in today's society is also of value to this process.

Suffering and death are a natural part of existence. In traditional cultures, suffering and death often occurred at home, in full view of loved ones. Even children witnessed their relatives transitioning between disease and death. In modern societies, the network of hospitals, nursing homes, and hospice care have dramatically reduced encounters with those who are terminally ill and suffering. Our concepts of death and dying are now derived from films, video games, and social media, and this leaves us woefully unprepared for the understanding and compassion we need when facing the final transition. Keeping your loved ones close, not excluding them from your struggles, is emotionally beneficial for them and you as well.

To find meaning in death is to find purpose in life. "To face death as a life process"—writes Audre Lorde—"what is there possibly left to fear? Who can ever really have power over me again?" A similar thought is expressed by Buddha: "Even death is not to be feared by one who has lived wisely." Holding onto life by extending suffering for a few more days becomes counterproductive. Passing, which is an inevitable part of life, is sanctified by Jesus. Entering into the Hands of God frees us from the agony of pain. As Jesus prepared his mother and his favorite disciple for life without him, we have to release the ties to the living. End-of-life support includes "permission" from our loved ones to let go. This permission should be given before the patient enters the stage when he is no longer fully aware of his or her surroundings. Physiological changes, such as body temperature, blood pressure, and pulse, might occur. Closer to death, there is often a transient renewal of energy and purpose. Periods of quiet dignity and grace may be interrupted by sudden awareness.

Finally, the breathing may change; hands and feet may become blotchy and purplish. The lips and nail beds might become bluish or purple, and lips may droop. The person usually becomes unresponsive with partially or semi-open eyes, without awareness of their surroundings. Listening to a familiar voice might still comfort a dying loved one. In death, the millions of pieces of memories that kept our life stitched together fall finally quiet.

ECHO

Come to me in the silence of the night;
Come in the speaking silence of a dream;
Come with soft rounded cheeks and eyes as bright
As sunlight on a stream;
Come back in tears,
O memory, hope, love of finished years.

O dream how sweet, too sweet, too bitter sweet,
Whose wakening should have been in Paradise,
Where souls brimfull of love abide and meet;
Where thirsting longing eyes
Watch the slow door
That opening, letting in, lets out no more.

Yet come to me in dreams, that I may live
My very life again though cold in death:
Come back to me in dreams, that I may give
Pulse for pulse, breath for breath:
Speak low, lean low
As long ago, my love, how long ago.

    By Christina Georgina Rossetti

WHAT WILL YOU GIVE?

What will you give
When death knocks at your door?

The fullness of my life-
The sweet wine of autumn days and summer nights,
My little board gleaned through the years,
And hours rich with living.

These will be my gift.
When death knocks at my door.
    By Rabindragath Tagore

STATION XII

Jesus Dies On the Cross

"Father, into thy hands I commend my spirit: and
having said thus, he gave up the ghost."

—LUKE 23:46 (KJB)

12, DEATH

"And if I go and prepare a place for you, I will come
back and take you to be with me that you also may be
where I am."

—JOHN 14:3 (NIV)

"For we know that if the earthly tent we live in is
destroyed, we have a building from God, an eternal
house in heaven, not built by human hands."

—2 CORINTHIANS 5:1 (NIV)

"The person, who dies in peace, with acceptance rather
than bitterness, bestows a gift upon the survivors,
which lasts for them, and can quieten their own fears."

—YOUNG AND CULLEN[7]

Following the Day after Pentecost, St. Peter declared to the crowds
in Solomon's Portico, "You rejected the Holy and Righteous One
and asked to have a murderer given to you, and you killed the
Author of life, who God raised from the dead. To this we are wit-
nesses."—Acts 3:14–15 (ESV)

Genesis 2:27 (NIV) describes the process of creation, the moment when mankind received the breath of life. Elsewhere in Genesis 1:7 (NIV), we find "God created man in His own image, in the
image of God He created him; male and female He created them."
Dualities appear in every aspect of life: male and female, body and
soul, brain and mind, life, and death. At the threshold of life and its
passing, we can reflect on the eternal value of life.

At the time of death, the sensory organs cease to operate. An
electric spike can be measured about 60 to 120 milliseconds after
the patient becomes pulseless. Without sensory interaction with the
outside world, death ensues. The loss of your material body frees the

7. Young and Cullen, *Good Death*. 162–63.

indestructible spiritual energy of your soul. Matthew 10:28 (NIV), "And do not fear those who kill the body but cannot kill the soul."

Prayer

> "Prayer is the most concrete way to make our home in God."
>
> —Henri Nouwen

Prayer is a type of meditation that utilizes the belief in a higher power as its focal point. The word prayer comes from the Latin phrase prex or precis, meaning supplication to a Higher Power that transcends the material space. Religious rituals and prayer are an organic part of human existence and have been since ancient times. Touching the icon of a benevolent saint, prayer with rosary beads, and saying the holy liturgy at Mass are ways in which Christian prayers are performed. Jesus instructs us not to pray to impress others but to connect to our Father in Heaven (Matthew 6:5–15). The humbleness of private prayer is favored over public displays of piety.

In our modern world, personal and existential worries indicate a hunger for meaning and purpose. Without belief, we become skeptics—we need a referral and official papers for validation. For a person with faith, the belief in a higher power is instrumental in making things happen. It is hard to argue with the Buddhist view that the self is always changing. How can prayer remain a steady force amid constant change? Can the will of God be influenced through prayer? These and similar questions maintain a timeless mystery for the faithful.

Personal guidance from a spiritual adviser can help clarify your perspective. Like meditation, prayer forms steadfast beliefs that support goals and the betterment of the self. Hope is interconnected with meaningful work and decency, and it cannot exist without it. An honest effort fuels inner strength, which permits "inherent knowing." These mental changes are the most critical, elevating outcomes of prayer. Trust in a higher power creates a mindset that is not afraid to fail. Fearlessness is a calm and trusting mental state, which succeeds in its objectives.

The Power of Prayer

Proximity to God allows believers to cope in times of illness and crisis better. Religious practices, such as prayer, are often associated with improved physical and mental health, immune function, welfare, life satisfaction, hope, optimism, and lower rates of anxiety and depression. Asking for good health and relief from illness was probably one of the earliest uses of prayer. Today, a renewed interest in prayer recognizes its power in holistic medicine as a complementary option to traditional therapy. Petition Prayer, which asks help for oneself, is different from Intercessory Prayer, which seeks benefit for another person. In Intercessory Prayer, there is no direct contact between the person offering the invocation and the recipient.

Prayer is often used by patients to facilitate the recovery process and promote well-being. It also fosters hope and strengthens belief in the sacred and self-transcending dimension. Prayer reduces the anxiety of patients undergoing chemotherapy, radiation, and other treatments. Thus, religious leaders or chaplains are considered members of the multidisciplinary healthcare team.

I FELT A FUNERAL, IN MY BRAIN, (340)

I felt a Funeral, in my Brain,
And Mourners to and fro
Kept treading—treading—till it seemed
That Sense was breaking through -

And when they all were seated,
A Service, like a Drum -
Kept beating—beating—till I thought
My mind was going numb -

And then I heard them lift a Box
And creak across my Soul
With those same Boots of Lead, again,
Then Space—began to toll,

As all the Heavens were a Bell,
And Being, but an Ear,
And I, and Silence, some strange Race,
Wrecked, solitary, here -

And then a Plank in Reason, broke,
And I dropped down, and down -
And hit a World, at every plunge,
And Finished knowing—then -
     By Emily Dickinson

ELEGY TO THE OLD MAN HOKUJU

You left in the morning, at evening my heart is in a
thousand pieces.
Why is it so far away?

Thinking of you, I go up on the hill and wander.
Around the hill, why is it such a sadness?

Dandelions yellow and shepherds-purse blooming white —
not anyone to look at them.

I hear a pheasant, calling and calling fervently.
Once a friend was there across the river, living.

Ghostly smoke rises and fades away with a west wind
strong in fields of small bamboo grasses and reedy fields.
Nowhere to leave for.

Once a friend was there across the river, living, but today
not even a bird sings a song.

You left in the morning, at evening my heart is in a
thousand pieces.
Why is it so far away?

In my grass hut by the Amida image I light no candle,
offer no flowers, and only sit here alone.
This evening, how invaluable it is.

> By Priest Buson
> with a thousand bowings

STATION XIII

Jesus Is Taken Down From the Cross

"I am poured out like water, and all my bones are out
of joint: My heart is like wax; it is melted in the midst
of my bowels."

—PSALM 22:14 (KJV)

13, PREPARATION FOR INTERMENT

"Consider and hear me O Lord my God lighten mine
eyes, lest I sleep the sleep of death."

—PSALM 13: 3 (KJB)

"For you were made from dust, and to dust you will
return."

—GENESIS 3:19 (NLT)

Following the death of Jesus, we find one of the most poignant
scenes about love and caring at the foot of the Cross. Jesus' followers lovingly take his body down from the Cross and wrap it in a
clean linen shroud. These good works are carried out by loved ones
of the deceased as they prepare for the funeral.

Rituals are a natural part of religious, cultural, national, or individual identity and form an elemental part of a stable society. The
repetitive and sacred actions are highly meditative and constitute
an automatic repertoire for the mind. Traditions channel the raw
feelings of grief into rituals, which redirects the painful emotions
toward belonging. The sacred, customary practices form a powerful
bond from the past to the future.

Preparing for the funeral service often serves to strengthen relationships among family members. The funeral is a celebration of
the deceased's legacy as part of the cherished heritage of the family
and community. Following our loved one's bequest can give a sense
of comfort and accomplishment to the family. Funerals also serve
as a way for us to commend a loved one to one's creator. It is an
essential work for the family, loved ones, and friends. As we "make
the handoff to God," we release a person into God's safekeeping.

Jesus, a teacher, philosopher, a courageous man of faith and
confidence in himself and his ministry, focused on helping people.
As the forerunner of Christianity, he embraced everyone independent of their affiliation, religion, sex, race, and conventions. He
revolutionized the way we view ourselves (the son of God) and how

we relate to each other (brothers and sisters). In death, we become part of His family in a real sense. His teachings had turned a pagan ritual into a celebration of God's power. But his revolution is still not complete; his words are still relevant, and we are still in need of transformation. Jesus' teachings and deeds are relayed to us by his disciples in the Gospels of the Bible.

Science and religion often seem in contradiction with each other. Nevertheless, ultimately they both examine the mystery of existence. We can rely on science in the matters of the body, but faith takes over in the questions of the soul. The Scriptures point out that life forms the bridge between matter and the intelligence of God: "The Spirit of God has made me, and the breath of the Almighty gives me life," Job 33:4 (NIV). Religion allows us to view God as the infinite generosity and promise of the universe. Our bodies are material, but our minds are the living reflection of the cosmos, the spiritual realm of God. The immense potential of our spirit prevails over our fragile material bodies. Ashes to ashes, dust to dust, but our soul lives on.

REMEMBER

Remember me when I am gone away,
Gone far away into the silent land;
When you can no more hold me by the hand,
Nor I half turn to go yet turning stay.
Remember me when no more day by day
You tell me of our future that you plann'd:
Only remember me; you understand
It will be late to counsel then or pray.
Yet if you should forget me for a while
And afterwards remember, do not grieve:
For if the darkness and corruption leave
A vestige of the thoughts that once I had,
Better by far you should forget and smile
Than that you should remember and be sad.

By Christina Georgina Rossetti

GRADUAL (4 ESDRAS 2:34–35; PSALM 111:7)

Eternal rest give unto them, O Lord;
and let perpetual light shine upon them.
The just shall be in everlasting remembrance;
he shall not fear the evil hearing.

STATION XIV

Jesus Is Placed in the Tomb

"But God will redeem my soul from the power of the grave: for he shall receive me."

—PSALMS 49:15 (NKJV)

14, TAKEN TO THE TOMB (FUNERAL)

"Be afflicted, and mourn, and weep, let your laughter
be turned to mourning, and your Joy to heaviness."

—JAMES 4:9 (KJB)

"Caring for a mother who suffers from dementia was
really hard. I wish I could do it again."

—MELANIE BISHOP[8]

Jesus was born in a manger and died on the cross. Both his birth
and his death relied on the grace of others. Jesus' burial in a donated
Tomb brings his life full circle. Mary and Joseph held him close at
his humble birth, and now Joseph of Arimathea, Nicodemus, Mary
Magdalene, and others gather around him. Dictated by Jewish cus-
tom, his burial occurs within 24 hours of death. After the Sabbath,
the women bring spices to his tomb to anoint the body; we can
envision the similarity to the visitation of Magi from the East, who
brought frankincense, gold, and myrrh.

Emotions take a form that is unique to the situation and the
individual. This is the same for grief. We can never tell beforehand
for whom and how we will suffer through it. The duties in prepara-
tion for the funeral keep the sadness at bay. Holding on to the belief
in life beyond the grave can ease the pain. After the services, when
the well-wishers depart, the family is left with the emptiness and
bereavement. The heartache might be similar to the grief felt by the
patient at the time of diagnosis. We have come full circle.

Questions of Afterlife

"For whatsoever a man soweth, that shall he also reap."

—GALATIANS 6:7 (ASV)

---

8. Bishop. *New York Times.*

Death extinguishes the relentless flow of signals from the sensory organs and, with it, the loud chatter of the neural tissue. The end of biological life frees our limitless soul from our material bodies. Death begins the soul's timeless journey. For people with a debilitating disease, the separation is liberation from pain and suffering. Your personal emotional history, the way you lived your mortal life, forms your spiritual afterlife. A self-centered existence, when we cannot separate our soul from our egoistic desires, generates a cosmic journey toward hell. Self-centered people look at life from a personal point of view. Their distorted self-evaluation exaggerates their self-importance. Whether we push ourselves down (I do not deserve to be happy, I am not good enough) or elevate ourselves above others, it falsifies our genuine self.

Matthew 5:22 (MIV): ". . . whosoever shall say, Thou fool, shall be in danger of hell fire." Hell is dark, hot, and non-moving. In this tight confinement, time is frozen, still, and thralled with heaviness. The absence of space halts all movement, leaving everything beyond approach. We cannot even reach out to our next-door neighbor, the curse of loneliness in a crowded world.

Only by accepting our whole life with humble devotion to God can we transform transgressions and sin into a blessing. According to Matthew 12:33 (BSB), a tree is known for its fruit. Likewise, Matthew 12:35 (NIV) says: "A good man brings good things out of the good stored up in him, and an evil man brings evil things out of the evil stored up in him." Like a good tree, the grace of salvation fills the soul with love that moves it toward the light of heaven. According to Romans 8:30 (ESV): "And those whom he predestined he also called, and those whom he called he also justified, and those whom he justified he also glorified."

The expanding, limitless potential of heaven is manifest in Jesus' words, "my Father's house has many rooms," John 14:2 (NIV). The soul becomes part of the expanding future of the cosmos. Revelation 7:16 (NIV) "Never again will they hunger; never again will they thirst. The sun will not beat down on them,' nor any scorching heat." Nevertheless, we learn in Revelation 22:5 (NET): "And night will be no more. They will need no light of lamp or sun, for the Lord God will be their light, and they will reign forever and ever." Heaven's unquenchable and limitless energy is a cold light that spreads the glory and power of God.[9]

Matthew 22:28–30 (NIV) highlights another aspect of heaven: "Now then, at the resurrection, whose wife will she be of the seven, since all of them were married to her?" Jesus replied, "You are in error because you do not know the Scriptures or the power of God. At the resurrection, people will neither marry nor be given in marriage; they will be like the angels in heaven." The disappearance of our personal characteristics is complete. The soul unclothed its selfishness and memories.

Revelation 3:21 (NIV), "Those who are victorious will sit with me on my throne, just as I was victorious and sat with my Father on his throne." The Scripture's promise is for the deserving soul to sit at the right hand of the father. The infinitely expanding space of heaven provides room for all to be neighborly. Jesus repeatedly assures us, "My Father's house has many rooms; if that were not so, would I have told you that I am going there to prepare a place for you?" John 14:2–3 (NIV). Jesus prepares a place of peace, joy, and infinite possibilities. In the loss of your individuality, your real power is liberated to participate in God's joyous work.

The richness and limitless potential of heaven is now your rightful destiny. The soul's painless peace is God's safekeeping. Thou art in Heaven.

9. Deli, *JCER*, 910–930.

SONG

When I am dead, my dearest,
Sing no sad songs for me;
Plant thou no roses at my head,
Nor shady cypress tree:
Be the green grass above me
With showers and dewdrops wet;
And if thou wilt, remember,
And if thou wilt, forget.
I shall not see the shadows,
I shall not feel the rain;
I shall not hear the nightingale
Sing on, as if in pain:
And dreaming through the twilight
That doth not rise nor set,
Haply I may remember,
And haply may forget.

By Christina Rosetti

VERSE 52 FROM "SONG OF MYSELF"

"The spotted hawk swoops by and accuses me, he complains of my gab and my loitering.

I too am not a bit tamed, I too am untranslatable,

I sound my barbaric yawp over the roofs of the world.

The last scud of day holds back for me,

It flings my likeness after the rest and true as any on the shadow'd wilds,

It coaxes me to the vapor and the dusk.

I depart as air, I shake my white locks at the runaway sun,

I effuse my flesh in eddies, and drift it in lacy jags.

I bequeath myself to the dirt to grow from the grass I love,

If you want me again look for me under your boot-soles.

You will hardly know who I am or what I mean,

But I shall be good health to you nevertheless,

And filter and fibre your blood.

Failing to fetch me at first keep encouraged,

Missing me one place search another,

I stop somewhere waiting for you."

By Walt Whitman

STATION XV

Hope

"But the fruit of the Spirit (Hope) is love, joy, peace, forbearance, kindness, goodness, faithfulness, gentleness and self-control."

—GALATIANS 5:22 (NIV)

15, AN EVER-PRESENT FUTURE

"Man has subjected himself to thousands of self-
inflicted bondages. Wisdom comes to a man who lives
according to the true eternal laws of nature."

—HOLY VEDAS[10]

"I can do everything through him who gives me
strength."

—PHILIPPIANS 4:13(NIV)

"The end of spring
Lingers
In the cherry blossoms."

—YOSA BUSON

Death does not cause hopelessness; instead, the lack of hope causes death. This last chapter is not part of the "official" Stages. However, it brings the stations full circle. Two of the most often used words in both the Bible and this book are "meaning" and "love." Love is a source of happiness, spiritual fulfillment, and prosperous life, being accepted and loved by the people closest to us and leading a meaningful existence. "I have learned to be content whatever the circumstances" Philippians 4:11 (NIV).

In 1 Corinthians 15:53 (ESV), Apostle Paul celebrates the resurrection with optimism and hope. According to Rom.6:3–5 (NIV), "Or don't you know that all of us who were baptized into Christ Jesus were baptized into his death? We were therefore buried with him through baptism into death in order that, just as Christ was raised from the dead through the glory of the Father, we too may live a new life. For if we have been united with him in a death like his, we will certainly also be united with him in a resurrection like his."

---

10. Satyakam Vidyalankar, *Holy Vedas.*

Breakthrough treatments for chronic diseases are at hand; every day brings us closer to some form of Cure. The most significant accomplishment is to go through the illness by growing in wisdom and to see life from a higher plane. In mythology, the Phoenix is reborn from the ashes of its own body. Cathartic events and experiences can inspire self-discovery. For a person of faith, there is hope, even in death.

In chronic diseases, staying ahead of the illness by being knowledgeable and aware of the latest research increases your chance of survival. Survival continually requires embracing change. Taking care of your body and soul is the best way to manage your life. Cancer survivors might struggle with the fear of recurrence. Nevertheless, fear should not rule your life.

Follow-up visits are a must. Eating a healthy diet, taking time to exercise, and finding activities with meaning will give you back your stamina and increase the will to live. Social connections and support groups, whether in your community or online, provide a platform to share your feelings and hear from others with similar experiences.

Spontaneous Remissions

"For many are called, but few chosen."

—Matthew 20:16 (NKJV)

"My mission in life is not merely to survive, but to thrive; and to do so with some passion, some compassion, some humor, and some style. Surviving is important. Thriving is elegant."

—Maya Angelou

"Do just once what others say you can not do and you will never pay attention to their limitations again."

—James R. Cook

For centuries and perhaps millennia, spontaneous remissions of chronic disease have been documented. Scientific estimates range to be about 1 in 100,000 cancers. However, the frequency of spontaneous regression of small tumors might be much higher. In one carefully controlled study, 22 percent of all breast cancer cases underwent spontaneous regression. Jesus certainly would support that conclusion. He regularly performed miraculous cures from diseases. Jesus' mother, who saw him growing up, always believed in her son's miraculous abilities. For the apostles, every miracle came out of the blue. For us, a cure must start by following traditional treatments; alternative approaches may provide additional benefits as well.

Spontaneous regression has been attributed to spiritual, immune, and other causes. Many cancer regressions appear to follow infections. Because an inflammatory response is necessary for healing, the infection-induced fever may stimulate the immune system. In other cases, dramatic lifestyle changes, or spiritual transformations preceded remission. Such transitions can lead to epiphanies, which enhance the zest for life. The enthusiasm for life contributes to healing. Whether you are successful in your effort, there is nobility in the struggle to change in the hope of a better tomorrow. David Smithers, professor of radiology and a leading cancer specialist, found that a dramatic positive turn in the patient's social environment might be a pivotal catalyst to healing.

O'Regan and Hirshberg[11] at the Institute of Noetic Sciences have documented the attributes of spontaneous remission or regression. Not surprisingly, their suggestions are congruent with the recommendations in this book. Their outstanding work summarizes practices for patients that might boost the efficiency of medical treatment.

1. A change from dependency to autonomy combined with act attitudes and behaviors that promote increased autonomy, awareness of themselves, others, and their environment, love, joy, play, satisfaction, laughter, and humor.

11. O'Regan and Hirshberg, *Spontaneous remission.*

2. Facing the crisis, the despair, the sadness, and the pain and discovering they have the power to find a new way of life that is fulfilling and meaningful.
3. Taking control of their lives (personal, and professional, emotional, spiritual, and medical), and living each day fully combined with a willingness to evaluate their beliefs and attitudes and change the old beliefs and attitudes that are no longer appropriate or adequate.
4. Becoming comfortable with and expressing and accepting both their positive and negative emotions/feelings, their needs, wants, and desire (physical, emotional, spiritual) and the ability to say "No" when it is necessary for their wellbeing.
5. Having at least one strong loving relationship, an activity, an organization(s), changing the quality of their interpersonal relationships with spouses, friends, family, neighbors, doctors, nurses, etc. in a positive way, and/or motivation to help others.
6. Working in partnership with their physicians and participating in decisions related to their health and wellbeing.
7. Finding meaning in the experience of cancer, finding reasons to live, accepting the diagnosis but not the prognosis, seeing the disease as a challenge, belief in a positive outcome, and having a renewed desire, will, and commitment to life.
8. Choosing activities and practices that promote increased awareness and reduce stress (imagery, stress reduction, yoga, etc.); showing renewed spiritual awareness (Soul) that often results in spiritual practice (prayer, meditation, religious affiliation, connection to nature, etc.).

"HOPE" IS THE THING WITH FEATHERS—(314)

"Hope" is the thing with feathers -
That perches in the soul -
And sings the tune without the words -
And never stops—at all -

And sweetest—in the Gale—is heard -
And sore must be the storm -
That could abash the little Bird
That kept so many warm -

I've heard it in the chillest land -
And on the strangest Sea -
Yet—never—in Extremity,
It asked a crumb—of me.
        By Emily Dickinson

DREAMS

Hold fast to dreams
For if dreams die
Life is a broken-winged bird
That cannot fly.
Hold fast to dreams
For when dreams go
Life is a barren field
Frozen with snow.

By Langston Hughes

Afterword

My parents were my first teachers, and their wisdom has guided me throughout all my struggles and successes. Their simple life made up in dignity and generosity what it lacked in material riches. My father passed away three decades earlier than my mother. She was a simple seamstress, but her intellect and humanity were evident in her every action. She was a well-liked and respected member in the neighborhood, but her love and endless desire to help was most apparent for her family, her children, and grandchildren. As a seamstress, she could create colorful wall hangings from old clothes and pieces of fabric, or tailor fashionable dresses. Despite her busy schedule, she was never too busy to alter my dress or repair her grandson's jeans. Her simple upbringing on a traditional Hungarian farm was not a disadvantage for her in writing poetry.

She made sure we attended Sunday Mass every week. Attending Mass was just as much a natural ritual as my mother's four-course dinner. She took pride in preparing it from scratch. She started her signature chicken stew before she left for the service. As the time to gather around the dinner table approached, the kitchen was filled with the sweet fragrance of homemade pastry or cake.

Her service to others with selfless abandon and dignity inspired us to value education and community. When she developed cancer, I went to live with her. In the last years of her life, she recounted many stories of the simple life on her childhood farm. This was an immense comfort for both of us, and I cherish those memories.

She carried herself with dignity and kindness even at the latest stages of the disease.

Bibliography

Albertine, Viv. *Clothes, Clothes, Clothes. Music, Music, Music. Boys, Boys, Boys.: A Memoir*. New York: Faber and Faber. 2019.

Armstrong-Coster, Angela. *Living and Dying with Cancer*. New York: Cambridge University Press. 2004.

Bishop, Melanie. *I Would Have Driven Her Anywhere. Caring for a mother who suffers from dementia was really hard: I wish I could do it again*. The New York Times. 2018.

Deli, E. "Consciousness, a cosmic phenomenon—A hypothesis." *Journal of Consciousness Exploration & Research*. 7:11 (2016) 910–30.

Kubler-Ross, Elisabeth. *On death and dying* (40th anniversary ed.). Abingdon, UK: Routledge. 2009.

Lewis, C.S. *Letter to Mary Willis Shelburne*. June 17, 1963.

Nhat Hanh, Thich. *Stepping into Freedom: An Introduction to Buddhist Monastic Training. Berkeley, California*. Parallax Press. 2001.

O'Regan, B., and Hirshberg, C. *Spontaneous remission*. An Annotated Bibliography. Sausalito: Institute of Noetic Sciences. 1993.

Satyakam Vidyalankar, Pandit. *The Holy Vedas*. New York: Clarion. 1998.

Yalom, Irvin D, ed. *Rachel E. Menzies Curing the Dread of Death: Theory, Research and Practice*. Samford Valley, Australia: Australian Academic Press. 2018.

Young, Michael and Cullen, Lesley. *A Good Death: Conversations with East Londoners*. London, UK: Routledge. 1996.

Resources

PRAYER AND SPIRITUAL PRACTICES

Anderson, J. W. & Nunnelley, P. A. "Private prayer associations with depression, anxiety and other health conditions: an analytical review of clinical studies." *Postgraduate medicine* 128 (2016) 635–641.

Vitorino, L.M., Lucchetti, G. et al. "The association between spirituality and religiousness and mental health." *Sci Rep* 8 (2018) 17233.

Andrade, Chittaranjan and Radhakrishnan, R. "Prayer and healing: A medical and scientific perspective on randomized controlled trials." *Indian J Psychiatry.* 51 (2009) 247–53.

Büssing, A., Frick, E. et al. "Health and Life Satisfaction of Roman Catholic Pastoral Workers: Private Prayer has a Greater Impact than Public Prayer." *Pastoral Psychol* 65 (2016) 89–102.

Harding, S. R., Flannelly, K. J. et al. "The influence of religion on death anxiety and death acceptance." *Mental Health, Religion & Culture*, 8:4 (2005) 253–261.

Johnston Taylor, Elizabeth. "Health Outcomes of Religious and Spiritual Belief, Behavior, and Belonging: Implications for Healthcare Professionals." In *Spirituality in Healthcare: Perspectives for Innovative Practice.* edited by Timmins, Fiona, Caldeira, Sílvia. 67–82. New York. Springer. 2019.

Krause, N. and Hayward, R. D. "Prayer beliefs and change in life satisfaction over time." *Journal of religion and health*, 52(2) (2013) 674–694.

Lipira, L. Williams, E. C. et al. "Religiosity, Social Support, and Ethnic Identity." *JAIDS* 81:2 (2019) 175–183.

O'Connell-Persaud, S. Dehom, S. et al. "Online Survey of Nurses' Personal and Professional Praying." *Holistic Nursing Practice* 33:3 (2019) 131–140.

Simão TP, Caldeira, S. et al. "The effect of prayer on patients´ health: systematic literature review." *Religions* 7 (2016) 11.

Vitorino, L.M., Lucchetti, G. et al. "The association between spirituality and religiousness and mental health." Sci Rep 8 (2018) 17233.

Visser, A., Garssen, B. et al. Spirituality and well-being in cancer patients: A review. Psycho-Oncology, 19, (2010). 565-–72.

Grezsta, E. and Sieminska, M. J. "Patient-perceived changes in the system of values after cancer diagnosis." *J Clin Psychol.* 18 (2011) 55–64.

SPONTANEOUS REMISSIONS

Engebretson, J., Peterson, N. et al. "Exceptional Patients: Narratives of Connections." *Palliative and Supportive Care* 12:4 (2014) 29–276.

Haruki, T., Makamura, H. et al. "Spontaneous Regression of Lung Adenocarcinoma: Report of a Case." *Surgery Today* 40:12 (2010) 1155–8.

Jessy, T. "Immunity over Inability: The Spontaneous Regression of Cancer." *Journal of Natural Science, Biology, and Medicine* 2:1 (2011) 43–49.

Zahl, P., Maehlen, J. et al. "The Natural History of Invasive Breast Cancers Detected by Screening Mammography." *Archives of Internal Medicine* 168:21 (2008) 2311–6.

STRESS AND DEPRESSION

Lorenz, L. Doherty, A.M. et al. "The Role of Religion in Buffering the Impact of Stressful Life Events on Depressive Symptoms in Patients with Depressive Episodes or Adjustment." Disorder. *International Journal of Environmental Research and Public Health* 16:7 (2019) 1238.

Yaribeygi, H., Panahi, Y. et al. "The impact of stress on body function: A review." *EXCLI journal, 16* (2017) 1057–1072.

Nelson, C. J., Rosenfeld, B. et al. "Spirituality, religion, and depression in the terminally ill." *Psychosomatics* 43:3 (2002) 213–220.

END OF LIFE CARE

Breibart, W., Rosenfeld, B. et al. "Depression, hopelessness, and desire for hastened death in terminally ill patients with cancer." *JAMA* 284:22 (2000) 2907–11.

———. and Applebaum, A. Meaning-centered group psychotherapy. In *Handbook of psychotherapy in cancer care.* edited by M. Watson & D. Kissane 137–148. Chichester, England: Wiley, 2011.

Breitbart, W., and Poppito, S. *Individual meaning-centered psychotherapy for patients with advanced cancer: A treatment manual.* New York: Oxford University Press, 2014.

———., Rosenfeld, B. et al. "Meaning-centered group psychotherapy for patients with advanced cancer: A pilot randomized controlled trial." *Psycho-Oncology* 19:1 (2010) 21–28.

———. Poppito, S. et al. "Pilot randomized controlled trial of individual meaning-centered psychotherapy for patients with advanced cancer." *J Clin Oncol* 30:12 (2012) 1304–1309.

Chochinov, H. M., Hack, T. et al. "Dignity in the terminally ill: A cross-sectional, cohort study." *The Lancet* 360:9350 (2002) 2026–2030.

————., Kristjanson, L. J. et al.. "Effect of dignity therapy on distress and end-of-life experience in terminally ill: A randomised controlled trial." *The Lancet* 12 (2011) 753–762.

Cicirelli, V. G. *Older Adults' Views on Death.* New York: Springer, 2006.

————. "Personal meanings of death in older adults and young adults in relation to their fears of death." *Death Studies* 25:8 (2001) 663–683.

Fegg, M. J., Wasner, M. et al. "Personal values and individual quality of life in palliative care patients." *Journal of Pain and Symptom Management* 30:2 (2005) 154–159.

Gawande, Atul. *Being mortal: Medicine and what matters in the end.* Toronto, ON: Doubleday, 2014.

Gesser, G., Wong, P. T. P. et al. "Death attitudes across the life span. The development and validation of the Death Attitude Profile (DAP)." *Omega* 2 (1988) 113–128.

Greer, J. Jacobs, J. et al. "Role of Patient Coping Strategies in Understanding the Effects of Early Palliative Care on Quality of Life and Mood." *Journal of Clinical Oncology* 36:1 (2018) 53–60.

Hack, T., McClement, S. et al. "Learning from dying patients during their final days: Life reflections gleaned from dignity therapy." *Palliative Medicine* 24:7 (2010) 715–723.

Hartogh, GD. "Suffering and dying well: on the proper aim of palliative care." *Med Health Care Philos* 20:3 (2017) 413–424.

Hayes, S. C., Strosahl, K. D. et al. *Acceptance and commitment therapy.* New York: Guilford Press, 1999.

Iverach, L., Menzies, R. G. et al. "Death anxiety and its role in psychopathology: Reviewing the status of a transdiagnostic construct." *Clinical Psychology Review* 34:7 (2014). 580–593.

Jacobs, J., Greer, J. et al. "The Positive Effects of Early Integrated Palliative Care on Patient Coping Strategies, Quality of Life, and Depression." *Journal of Clinical Oncology* 35:31 (2017) 92.

Kastenbaum, Robert. *The psychology of death.* New York: Springer, 2000.

Kearl, Michael C. *Endings: A sociology of death and dying.* New York: Oxford University Press, 1989.

McClain, C., Rosenfeld, B. et al. "Effect of spiritual well-being on end-of-life despair in terminally-ill cancer patients." *The Lancet* 361 (2003) 1603–1607.

Moadel, A., Morgan, C. et al. "Seeking meaning and hope: Self-reported spiritual and existential needs among an ethnically diverse cancer patient population." *Psycho-Oncology* 8 (1999) 1428–1431.

Neimeyer, Robert A. ed. *Death anxiety handbook: Research, instrumentation, and application.* New York: Taylor & Francis, 1994.

Nipp, R., El-Jawahri, A. et al. "The Relationship Between Coping Strategies, Quality of Life and Mood in Patients With Incurable Cancer." *Cancer* 122:13 (2016) 2110–2116.

Pollak, K., Alexander, S. et al. "Physician empathy and listening: associations with patient satisfaction and autonomy." *JABFM* 24:6 (2011) 665–72.

Rokeach, Milton. *The nature of human values.* New York: Collier Maclillian, 1973.

Rome, RB, Luminais, HH. et al. "The role of palliative care at the end of life." *Ochsner J* 11:4 (2011) 348–52.

Tomer, A. ed. *Death attitudes and the older adult: Theories, concepts, and applications.* Philadelphia, PA: Brunner-Routledge, 2000.

———., Eliason, G. T. et al. *Existential and spiritual issues in death attitudes.* New York: Erlbaum, 2008.

Wholihan, D. "Seeing the Light: End-of-Life Experiences-Visions, Energy Surges, and Other Death Bed Phenomena." *Nurs Clin North Am* 51:3 (2016) 489–500.

Wong, P. T. P. and Tomer, A. "Beyond terror and denial: The positive psychology of death acceptance." *Death Studies*, 35:2 (2011) 99–106.

———., Carreno, D. F. et al. "Death acceptance and the meaning-centered approach to end-of-life care." In *Curing the dread of death: Theory, research and practice.* edited by Menzies, R. E., Menzies, R. G. and Iverach, L. 185–202. Samford Valley, Australia: Australian Academic Press, 2018.

———., Reker, G. T. et al. "Death Attitude Profile–Revised: A multidimensional measure of attitudes toward death." In *Death anxiety handbook: Research instrumentation and application.* edited by Neimeyer, R. A. (121–148). Washington: Taylor & Francis, 1994.

———. Meaning management theory and death acceptance. In *Death attitudes: Existential & spiritual issues.* edited by Tomer, A., Grafton, E. and Wong, P. T. P. 65–87. Mahwah, NJ: Erlbaum, 2008.

———. "Meaning therapy: An integrative and positive existential psychotherapy." *Journal of Contemporary Psychotherapy* 40:2 (2010) 85–99.

Yalom, Irvin D. *Staring at the Sun: Overcoming the Terror of Death.* San Francisco, CA: Jossey-Bass, 2009.